Smart Writing

Smart Writing

Demonstrable and Measurable
Skills for Sophisticated Writing

John Mauk

BLOOMSBURY ACADEMIC
NEW YORK · LONDON · OXFORD · NEW DELHI · SYDNEY

BLOOMSBURY ACADEMIC

Bloomsbury Publishing Inc, 1359 Broadway, New York, NY 10018, USA
Bloomsbury Publishing Plc, 50 Bedford Square, London, WC1B 3DP, UK
Bloomsbury Publishing Ireland, 29 Earlsfort Terrace, Dublin 2, D02 AY28, Ireland

BLOOMSBURY, BLOOMSBURY ACADEMIC and the Diana logo are trademarks of Bloomsbury Publishing Plc

First published in the United States of America 2025

Copyright © Bloomsbury Publishing Inc, 2025

All rights reserved. No part of this publication may be: i) reproduced or transmitted in any form, electronic or mechanical, including photocopying, recording or by means of any information storage or retrieval system without prior permission in writing from the publishers; or ii) used or reproduced in any way for the training, development or operation of artificial intelligence (AI) technologies, including generative AI technologies. The rights holders expressly reserve this publication from the text and data mining exception as per Article 4(3) of the Digital Single Market Directive (EU) 2019/790.

Bloomsbury Publishing Inc does not have any control over, or responsibility for, any third-party websites referred to or in this book. All internet addresses given in this book were correct at the time of going to press. The author and publisher regret any inconvenience caused if addresses have changed or sites have ceased to exist, but can accept no responsibility for any such changes.

A catalog record for this book is available from the Library of Congress

ISBN: HB: 978-1-4758-7474-7
PBK: 978-1-4758-7475-4
ePDF: 979-8-7651-6110-4
eBook: 978-1-4758-7476-1

Typeset by Deanta Global Publishing Services, Chennai, India
Printed and bound in the United States of America

For product safety related questions contact productsafety@bloomsbury.com.

To find out more about our authors and books visit www.bloomsbury.com and sign up for our newsletters.

Contents

Introducing the Smart Moves 1

1 Seeking Complexity 15
- (1) Unpacking Broad Terms 16
- (2) Focusing the Questions 20
- (3) Making New Comparisons 23
- (4) Creating Context 25
- (5) Advanced Move: Denying the Usual Associations 27

2 Applying a Concept 33
- (1) Adopting Specific Language 34
- (2) Taking on the Big Concepts 36
- (3) Advanced Move: Transporting a Concept 39

3 Analyzing Arguments 43
- (1) Considering the Context 45
- (2) Analyzing the Reasoning 47
- (3) Analyzing the Writer/Speaker 48
- (4) Identifying Counterarguments, Concessions, Qualifiers 52
- (5) Analyzing the Audience 56
- (6) Advanced Move: Calling Out Unstated Reasons 58
- (7) Advanced Move: Calling Out the Quiet Argument 61

4 Justifying a Position 65
- (1) Adopting a Position and Purpose 66
- (2) Breaking Down the Reasons 67
- (3) Providing Evidence 71
- (4) Managing the Opposition 73
- (5) Advanced Move: Seeking Reasons for Reasons 73

5 Applying Sources 77
 (1) Applying a Supportive Source 78
 (2) Drawing from a Vital Source 79
 (3) Synthesizing Sources 83
 (4) Drawing from the Past 87
 (5) Trusting but Verifying 89
 (6) Citing Sources 91

6 Seeking Tension 95
 (1) Detecting Subtle Tension 96
 (2) Connecting to a Broader Tension 99
 (3) Advanced Move: Breaking Up Dualities 101

7 Inspecting the Terms 107
 (1) Detecting Inaccuracy 109
 (2) Detecting Quiet Associations 110
 (3) Proposing a Different Term 112
 (4) Advanced Move: Flipping the Terms 114
 (5) Advanced Move: Changing the Lens 115

8 Escaping the Status Quo 119
 (1) Acknowledging Shared Assumptions 120
 (2) Challenging Quiet Assumptions 123
 (3) Questioning the Maxims 125
 (4) Questioning Common Reasons 128
 (5) Advanced Move: Breaking Up Common Comparisons 129

9 Reflecting 133
 (1) Examining Past Assumptions 135
 (2) Describing New Thinking 137

10 Mapping the Moves 141
 Explanatory or Descriptive Projects 142
 Analytical Projects 145
 Argumentative Projects 149
 Reflective Projects 154

11 Assessing the Moves 157
   I. Argumentative Writing 158
   II. Analytical Writing 160
   III. Personal/Reflective Writing 162

Glossary of Moves 165

Introducing the Smart Moves

Writing teachers have multiple, and sometimes divergent, goals. We must teach grammar, mechanics, format, arrangement, coherence, writing genres, research processes, emerging technologies, syntax, and a strangely evasive quality called by many names. Depending on the school and department, this quality is characterized as *richness, sophistication, rigor, complexity, depth,* or *critical thinking*. In short, writing teachers at various grade levels have been charged with teaching students how to think. It's been a challenging mission, and it's prompted a question across institutions: how does one best imbue writing instruction with intellectual complexity?

While the effort is longstanding, even ancient, it's found new urgency in recent decades. Across institutions and states, learning outcomes often begin with the intellectual or *epistemic* dimension of writing. Assessment rubrics underscore this shared value. Teachers consistently privilege intellectual depth or complexity over all other aspects. Common rubric categories include a range of criteria that look like the following:

- The writing exhibits intellectual depth and curiosity.
- The writing shows a rigorous approach to the topic.
- The writer takes a sophisticated stance on the issue.
- Ideas are rich and fully developed.
- The writing exhibits critical thinking about the topic.

Apparently, this epistemic dimension is crucial, but the associated terms often add mystery and frustration to teaching, learning, assessing, and reporting. For example, it's difficult to demonstrate *rigor* (or its opposite), and even more difficult to assess it within any given piece of writing. The same goes for *depth, complexity, curiosity*, and *richness*. Describing, modeling, and assessing such qualities require nonstop and even unproductive effort. Some headway has been made with critical thinking models and related taxonomies, but critical thinking has not traveled smoothly into writing instruction. The qualities of critical thinking or individual *habits of mind* must still be translated into demonstrable forms that can be modeled, taught, and assessed. In short, despite progress and genuine effort, writing teachers still struggle to characterize, model, and assess the most valued qualities of writing.

This book is a brief distillation of strategies. It comes from my own work with students and from many talks with fellow teachers—in middle school, high school, and college classrooms. It is driven by a basic notion: the best way to make student writing more sophisticated (rich, deep, rigorous) is to teach that quality *directly*, to identify the most powerful writerly elements, name them, model them, prompt students to try them out, and celebrate *any* degree of success. In other words, this book has one main purpose: to help teachers with the most heavily weighted but most difficult category of writing instruction.

The specifics offered here are, hopefully, not evasive. They are identifiable rhetorical devices, or what I'll call *moves*, that get worked out in written passages. The goal in each chapter is to eradicate the mysteries of sophisticated writing—to offer samples, activities, and prompts that make student writing richer. In this sense, *Smart Writing* is not a book for those teaching only gifted, advanced, or highly skilled students. It's for all teachers trying desperately to help students with something that seems now universally valued.

On a personal note, I taught first-year college writing for twenty-five years. At different points, I also worked with middle and high school students, primarily in afterschool support programs. Through those years, I came to a few relevant conclusions: (1) When given specific guidance, samples, and instructional support, most students quickly advance. (2) No matter the grade level, students are quite adept at acquiring skills that are clearly presented. (3) If they are to thrive, students need more than broad assignment categories, for example, informative, argumentative, narrative. They need a repertoire, a menu of savvy moves that can be applied across assignment types. In my experience, students who struggle are those who see writing situations with a limited lens, who imagine only a few purposes: informing, arguing, or storytelling. Students who thrive develop a bigger vocabulary about writing. *Smart Writing*, I hope, provides some new language. It offers an array of moves that will make students more agile, more confident, and more aware of possibilities.

My own courses changed dramatically when I began foregrounding these moves. Over the years, I went from valuing the epistemic dimension of writing to teaching it directly. In my final years of on-campus teaching, I even made the moves within these chapters the primary content of my courses. Whenever possible, I made class sessions, assignments, and even discussion about the moves themselves. We talked openly about *unpacking broad terms, denying usual associations, seeking tension, breaking up dualities*, and so on. This emphasis resulted in students focusing on their own intellectual prowess, honing their own skills, and showing off their best examples. After all, students want to see themselves as smart, as capable of doing elevated work. They want to witness their own writing evolve in dramatic ways. They want to see and feel genuine progress. When they do, a host of other issues—related to confidence, persistence, attention, and participation—fade into the background.

Foregrounding the smart moves—making them the core of a writing curriculum—deeply impacts students who've felt marginalized by less direct methods. Imagine, for instance, an anxious student who's never succeeded in writing, who's felt inept at every turn, who's barely passed her previous courses. With some direct language, modeling, and practice, she pulls off a complex passage that describes a gray area in a normally black-and-white debate. She has successfully *broken up a duality*, something the best writers and thinkers across disciplines have done. Her teacher and classmates can celebrate that passage, and suddenly, she sees herself as a writer, not a struggling student but someone who can maneuver within an idea. That moment, which I've seen many times over the years, matters to that student. She has passed through a threshold of self-determination. While she, like all writers, will continue to stumble, she now knows something beyond the mysteries of eloquence, rules, and grammar conventions. Given guidance, she can do something heady and powerful in writing.

Each chapter of this book makes the point that smart writing is not a mystery. It's the result of learnable moves. For example, when a writer *examines a past assumption* (explained in Chapter 9), that intellectual process results in a certain, perhaps inevitable, degree of richness. The very process requires a level of mental engagement. The same goes for all the moves explained in this book. Whether it's *transporting a concept, changing the lens*, or *unpacking a broad term*, the act itself *is* good thinking. When writers make such moves, they will be doing something worthy. Even if their writing stumbles a bit—even if they don't stick the landing—they will do the kind of writerly stuff that happens in savvy blogs, newspaper articles, treasured speeches, and so on. Practically speaking, they will come closer to stated learning outcomes. In other words, they need not make the moves in exemplary fashion. If they come close, if they try them out and approximate the strategy, they will have accomplished something important.

As students practice the moves discussed in the chapters, they will also become better readers. Once they begin studying and applying these moves, they will see them in published nonfiction writing—in journalism, op-eds, informational, and argumentative texts across countless platforms and academic disciplines. They will recognize writers *transporting concepts, making new comparisons, denying usual associations, unpacking broad terms*, and so on. They will, no doubt, be more equipped to follow writers into those interesting thickets—into the intellectual places that constitute sophisticated public writing.

About Chapters 1–9

The chapters cover a broad range of writerly issues. Some are more familiar to teachers and students; others are fundamentals that get less attention in mainstream curricula:

1. Seeking Complexity
2. Applying a Concept
3. Analyzing Arguments
4. Justifying a Position
5. Applying Sources
6. Seeking Tension
7. Inspecting the Terms
8. Escaping the Status Quo
9. Reflecting

Chapter 5, for instance, involves the common practice of integrating secondary sources into a writing project. But hopefully, the chapter draws attention to some particularly powerful (and learnable) moves. In other words, I hope the chapter highlights distinct ways great writers manage sources. While some moves are fundamental, others are nuanced and quietly powerful.

Some chapters correspond to widely assigned projects. For instance, Chapter 4, Justifying a Position supports argumentative writing projects, any assignment that asks students to argue, debate, assert an opinion, propose a solution, or take a stance. The basic moves described in the chapter can be applied to all those assignment types: (1) adopt a position and purpose, (2) break down the reasons, (3) provide evidence, (4) manage the opposition, (5) seek reasons for reasons. Students will not necessarily hear other teachers and college instructors use all these labels. They may not hear teachers urge them to "seek tension" or "escape the status quo." But students will absolutely be rewarded for integrating these moves into their writing. They will see their own writing differently, and they will have more diverse moves for exploring ideas and crafting nuanced positions.

Other chapters correspond to qualities of writing—to that evasive dimension we teachers hope to inculcate in student projects. For instance, Chapter 1, "Seeking Complexity," includes a range of moves that are valued, even celebrated, but not usually assigned. In other words, teachers rarely prompt students into a formal assignment that *seeks complexity*. Instead, they assign an informative, argumentative, or reflective project and then grant value to student work that embodies complex thoughts. The chapter seeks to help teachers (and students) talk about complexity in writing. It breaks down that quality into five learnable moves: (1) unpacking broad terms, (2) focusing the questions, (3) making new comparisons, (4) denying the usual associations, and (5) creating context. The chapter does not make the case that all five moves are necessary—or that the five moves must be done in any order. Instead, the chapter simply offers these moves as the most direct way for a writer to seek complexity. They can be done in different ways, in different places, for different needs. Of course, the chapter also gives teachers some language to help students value complexity in the first place.

All chapters include the following elements:

- Introductions: Each begins with a brief explanation of the key moves. These introductions are written directly to teachers and give some context for their function.
- The Moves: After a brief opening section, chapters get directly to the moves themselves, the specific writerly strategies that students can apply in their own work. These sections are written in a writer's, not a teacher's, voice. For example, they discuss ways *we* can approach

ideas and passages. I hope this approach has two benefits: (1) that it makes the moves under consideration feel widely applicable, and (2) that it allows teachers to borrow directly from the book and integrate passages into their lessons if they choose.

- Sample Passages: Each move is illustrated with at least one sample. The topics are not important to the nature of the chapter or the moves themselves. Instead, the topics serve only to demonstrate possible applications of the moves.
- Activity Prompts: The chapters offer a range of activity prompts designed to help students try the key moves in an informal, low-stakes fashion. This often means small group discussion. If teachers find the prompts valuable, they can borrow directly from these pages. (Rather than speak to teachers *about* activities, I decided the activities themselves might hold more practical value for busy teachers.)
- Key Questions: Sections within each chapter also include key questions that students can apply to their own projects. Teachers may decide to assign them as pre-writing (or invention) strategies.
- Advanced Moves: Each chapter ends with an advanced move, something that teachers can reserve for some classes or some assignments. While these moves may seem, at first glance, highly nuanced, they are still learnable. In my experience, even the most tentative writing students can make headway with advanced moves if they are given direct guidance and support.

About Chapter 10, "Mapping the Moves"

Students benefit from knowing common organizational patterns. As readers, they can more readily comprehend, analyze, evaluate, and synthesize if they can follow the text itself—if they can walk along through paragraphs and understand the course of events. As writers, they can relax into the process and develop ideas if they know some common structures. Teachers of writing understand this well. When students are nervous about an assignment, it's often because they lack a readily available map of the journey. Literally, *they don't know where to go from here*. Those of us who have written many essays have built up a repertoire. Our anxieties are not necessarily bound up in organizational issues but in political or intellectual tangles.

Of course, many students easily adopt the five-paragraph organizational pattern. It's taught across grade levels and comes in handy for a range of writing assignments, especially written exam responses. The paragraph formula remains consistent:

- A broad introduction that ends with a thesis (divided into three chunks).
- Supporting paragraph 1
- Supporting paragraph 2
- Supporting Paragraph 3
- A conclusion that rewords the thesis.

For years, some writing instructors—especially those in first-year college classrooms—have lamented the five-paragraph structure. They urge students to avoid it, not because they hate the number five or because they want students to be uncomfortable, but because *it limits what writers can do*. As a form, it invites writers to imagine topics as always having, or needing, three points. It doesn't account for other complexities. Again, it's a perfectly reasonable tool and even has a valuable educational function, but if students are learning more sophisticated intellectual moves, they also need more organizational patterns that dramatize those moves. They need options.

When writers steer toward insights—when they work toward sophistication and depth—they take on a certain level of risk. As the water deepens, the potential peril increases. Heavy ideas can slow down progress or drag a writer under. However, if they know the moves, if they know some arrangement strategies, and if they've seen how other writers handle the deep water, they're far more likely to keep on moving, to enter streams of thought, and to find the currents leading to new and better ideas.

Even the most earnest students often face undue anxiety because they have developed sophisticated ideas but lack viable strategies for charting out those ideas. When prompted to write, they are stymied by the gap between their nuanced thinking and the organizational patterns they've acquired. They often do not know the structural possibilities, so they ask for samples, for models that do something other than the five-paragraph path. When they plead for samples, they simply want to imagine a way forward. They want to lean into the writerly experience. In rhetorical terms, they need to bridge the possibilities of thinking and the possibilities of arrangement. If they are gaining intellectual complexity, they require a range of common but powerful organizational structures.

Chapter 10 addresses this need. It will help students engage a range of options. The section is filled with outlines—arrangement tools that students can use for structuring ideas. These outlines are not meant to be restrictive or limiting. Instead, they are meant to be generative: ways to get students thinking without the terrifying uncertainty of *where to go next*.

About Chapter 11, "Assessing the Moves"

This section offers practical advice (along with sample rubrics) for measuring student work. The book operates on the simple notion that teaching and assessment are necessarily coupled, not only in the classroom but also in the lounge and administrative office. Teachers must account for their lessons. They must track and show progress. Most importantly, they must give students specific criteria used in determining grades. *Smart Writing* offers criteria, sample rubrics, and rationale for each.

About Invention

Modern writing pedagogy emerged from the ancient study of rhetoric, the disciplinary field created by Greek sophists and later teachers such as Aristotle and Cicero. Originally, rhetoric included five categories or canons of study: invention, arrangement, style, delivery, and memory. As the study of rhetoric morphed into the study of writing (over millennia), the first canon, invention, was stripped away. What was once the first and most important part of rhetoric slid into other content areas or disappeared altogether. Writing pedagogy entered the nineteenth and twentieth centuries with an intense focus on structure and style. As many theorists have argued, the disappearance or diminishment of invention undercut the power, even the purpose, of writing instruction. Invention, they have argued, was the single most impactful and worthy canon.

Invention was characterized as a complex intellectual process in which one seeks out "the most available means of persuasion." In practical terms, invention was a process of generating something to say—especially something designed for the occasion. In more elaborate terms, invention was a process of generating increasingly valuable insights—increasingly sophisticated insights. The Greeks, then, believed students of the craft could acquire specific moves that helped them to invent ideas. Coming up with something fresh, witty, effective, or powerful wasn't driven by divine inspiration (or caffeine intake) but by specific instruction. There were huge taxonomies of moves—categories and subcategories for creating complex and forceful speeches. Unfortunately, modern writing pedagogy largely abandoned those tools and replaced them with "brainstorming." Of course, the practical problem with brainstorming is that it helps students who are already comfortable with writing. It often stumps the least comfortable, the least verbal. Also, *brainstorming*, the term itself, suggests a chaotic and unpredictable storm of activity in the brain, not a deliberate and learnable process for generating ideas. If lightning strikes once, it likely won't hit in the same place or in the same fashion. In short, the assumptions at the heart of *brainstorming* are unhelpful to students. The term teaches *the exact wrong thing* about writing—how it works, how it doesn't, how to get better.

For these reasons, I've argued vehemently against brainstorming and all its strange curricular siblings that add mystery and awkwardness to writing. It's high time for brainstorms to pass. Students deserve the most direct, repeatable, learnable, and impactful strategies for generating ideas. The moves offered in this book are, I hope, the opposite of brainstorming. They are invention techniques in the classic sense. When applied, they help writers generate their own passages—no matter the topic, no matter the assignment.

About Reading

As students acquire the moves in this book, they will begin recognizing them in written published texts. In other words, they will see how other writers *unpack terms, break down reasons, manage opposition*, and so on. As that happens, they will become better readers—more able to follow texts into intellectual thickets. But teachers can help the process along with ancillary assignments that invite students to find published articles (from news magazines or their favorite online outlets) and identify the most impactful moves. Such assignments can be carried out in pairs or small groups. The important element is seeking out passages in which published authors unpack terms, make new comparisons, break down reasons, counterargue points, and so on. With only a few such examples, students will begin to see how these moves go far beyond school.

The moves presented in the chapters show up in countless textual categories or genres—reports, essays, op-eds, memoirs, and reports. In other words, *Smart Writing* makes a subtle post-genre case: writers make a range of familiar moves across text types and writerly situations. However, students also benefit from some basic (or not-so-basic) training in genre. As consumers of online information, they interact with a broad range of genres—many of which are not marked or curated for educational purposes. In other words, students encounter a sea of textuality without clear signs or distinctions. They may read a blog post the same way they read a government report. Of course, they are not the same. They have vastly different purposes, audiences, and rhetorical nuances, but they may show up in the same feed or on the same platform. In fact, first-year college curricula across the country have addressed this phenomenon and now include *information literacy* outcomes, practices that help students understand the nature of online texts.

At its root, genre is about expectations. Genres establish what readers expect to happen. In the same way musical genres establish ensemble and song structure, writing genres establish rhetorical boundaries. People listening to a new country music hit do not expect to hear a tuba solo in the middle of the song. Instead, they expect to hear twangy guitars, steady drums, bass, slide guitar, a low male voice, a high female voice—and a range of more subtle elements related to lyrical content, song length, melodies, harmonies, and so on. This is not to say that individual songs or groups can't stray from the norm. Genres are not laws. They are categories that hold on over time and maintain certain expectations. They establish how audiences approach the subject matter.

The most direct way to help students manage the sea of online texts is to help them see different genres. Of course, genre theory gets quickly complicated, but it needn't. Students can benefit from brief explanations. If they understand some fundamental differences between a report and an op-ed, between a proposal and a memoir, they will have more readerly traction:

- Report: a detailed summary of events or gathered information. A report is primarily a means of conveying information. It tells what happened or what has already been concluded.
- Essay: an expression or demonstration of a complex idea. Essays walk through and portray sophisticated thinking. Their job in academia,

and in public life, is to help writers and readers think through an issue—not necessarily to conclude an issue or even to determine an action, but to understand it better. This is why the essay dominates so much college work—why writers in all disciplines publish essays.

- Proposal: a call to act on a specific situation. Proposals are often solutions to public problems or detailed suggestions for addressing a specific need. They take various forms depending on the audience—whether corporate, governmental, or academic readers are involved.

- Memoir: a personal account of one's own life. A memoir is like an autobiography but more selective. Rather than covering all layers and dimensions of one's life, a memoir homes in on a particular element or time in the writer's life and borrows selectively from other parts. For instance, a presidential memoir would recount school memories only if they ultimately shed some light on the presidential years.

- Profile: an examination of someone else's public role. Profiles are like memoirs, but they focus on someone other than the writer. They look selectively at a particular part of someone's life—usually the public part. A profile of a social worker would focus on his work with clients. A profile of a CEO would focus on her duties or actions in corporate life. Profiles can be short (written like an academic essay) or long (written in book format).

- Review: a summary and critique of a specific text or service. Reviews come in a huge range, the most popular or well-established being the book review and the movie review. Reviews are openly evaluative, which means the writer is making an argument about the worth of the book, movie, text, proposal, product, or venue. Reviewers, in a sense, make a case for others to read, see, use, or visit the item in question.

Of course, there are many more genres: manifestos, mission statements, press releases, elegies, and so on. And students are probably familiar with some of the common literary genres, such as sonnets, romance novels, and graphic novels. By virtue of living in a complex and highly networked society, students encounter many genres on a weekly basis, and they unconsciously know how to deal with them—at least some of them. And here's the tricky part: genres blur together. A proposal often comes in the form of an essay. Reviews sometimes include a layer of profile. Like musical styles—for example, blues-rock, jazz fusion, country-rock—writing genres blend together. Still, it's valuable to understand the above distinctions.

A Final Note

Given the emergence and increasing utility of artificial intelligence, writing instruction will change. AI language generators will, no doubt, become widely used in society—in industries across all sectors. Marketing, journalism, and editing have already embraced robotic language generators. So why teach students how to write? For those of us who've spent decades in classrooms, we have several good answers. We know, for instance, that writing is a place, perhaps the best place, for students to develop and hone crucial intellectual impulses. Writing is where and how students learn to make mental moves that carry them into an increasingly complex world. Writing in various genres develops students' inventiveness, reasoning, creativity, logic, and powers of conception.

At the end of the previous century, back when I started teaching at a community college, I surveyed rubrics from a range of schools and departments. I collected whatever teachers used to assess writing and assign grades. I wanted to see what others valued most: which aspects of writing they prioritized, which they put at the forefront of their teaching. That process taught me a great deal. Almost universally, the first and most heavily weighted rubric category was not related to structure, grammar, mechanics, or coherence but to epistemic qualities—all those mental operations that get enacted in scholastic prose. In follow-up discussions, I asked teachers to amplify their thoughts—to break down terms such as *depth*, *rigor*, and *sophistication*. Of course, we all knew the difficulty of that question. They understood the nature of my pursuit, and many of us talked at length (for hours, years, or decades) about the weirdly difficult processes of getting our writing students into productive intellectual thickets—beyond the shallows or what composition theorist Jasper Neel once called "anti-writing."

There are countless indirect ways to nudge students toward more sophisticated writing. We can assign increasingly complex reading and guide them from comprehension to application. We can reward sophistication and redirect its opposite. We can prompt students to follow mentor texts, to trace the precise steps of a great model. Most of us use a multifaceted approach, incorporating a slew of strategies to lead students further into syntactical, rhetorical, and conceptual complexity, and yet the effort often seems far greater than the effect.

As I note above, I've worked with students from middle school to college and beyond. Currently, I teach in an adult continuing education program. Again, and still, I have found that writers long for the most direct and most applicable strategies possible. When students say, in whatever language, "please, just show me what to do," I have taken them seriously. Students of all ages genuinely want to know how to do well. Whether it means they simply want a good grade, want to complete the assignment, or want to become published writers, students of all stripes want clarity of mission. They don't want to guess at the road to success. (Who does?) They want the keys to the writerly kingdom, and I believe teachers should do whatever possible to grant them access.

1 Seeking Complexity

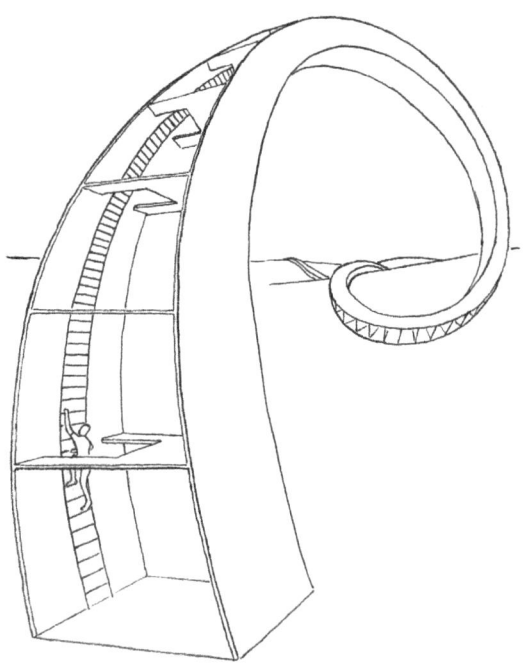

Popular culture celebrates speedy answers. Game shows pay out big money for contestants who can buzz in quickly, talk shows feature rapid-fire shouting matches between commercial breaks, and plenty of cop shows make it seem as though mysteries can be solved within a few days. It's not only popular culture that celebrates speed. The education industry sometimes supports the fast-answer regime with standardized tests that require students to answer quickly and move to the next question. In other words, students are surrounded by a culture that encourages having, spouting, or marking the right answer. However, writing well often means holding off on fast answers and preformed opinions. In fact, easy answers—*any* answers—can undermine good writing. They can keep writers from exploring the quiet corners of thought. They can short-circuit the logical powers that promote exploration.

If they are to grow as writers and thinkers, students need messaging contrary to the fast-answer regime. They need to learn skills beyond quick-fire conclusions. They must learn that sophisticated writing requires a willingness to keep thinking—to keep climbing beyond initial opinions or beliefs. And they should know writers of all stripes often begin projects assuming they'll discover more than they already know.

This may all sound grand, too grand for young or apprehensive writers. Seeking complex ideas can feel like wandering aimlessly. If students are uncertain, if they don't already know what they'll say, how to get started, or where they're headed, frustration can mount. This means assignments must accommodate their uncertainty and cultivate willingness. In other words, seeking complexity must be part of the curricular formula. Teachers must provide time and guidance. Fortunately, there are specific, learnable, and repeatable skills that can help young writers increase the complexity, depth, and sophistication of their work. This chapter offers five specific moves: (1) unpacking broad terms, (2) focusing the questions, (3) making new comparisons, (4) creating context, (5) denying the usual associations

(1) Unpacking Broad Terms

Broad terms are big. They don't refer to a specific person, place, or thing but to many or all in a category: *people*, *humanity*, *society*, *nature*, *the world*, *the government*, *knowledge*, *history*, *the past*, *the future*, *America*, *religion*, *liberalism*, *conservatism*, *Christianity*, *education*. Each of these terms (and countless others like them) operate in our daily lives. They're in headlines, journalism, social media, talk shows, news shows, and so on. In other words, it makes sense that broad terms like these would make their way into writing. And such terms are not inherently bad. They don't corrupt anyone's thinking, but relying on them can hold writers back. They can cause writers to generalize and, most importantly, miss interesting layers of a topic. When we rely on such terms, our brains go sailing over the top of important distinctions. But when we see the specifics within broad terms, we are less apt to fall victim to over-generalized statements and unsupportable arguments.

Broad terms like those above contain many smaller parts or elements. For example, consider *the government*—a phrase used in political debates. It's common to complain about *the government* as though one group of people is responsible for everything from local sewers to nuclear energy policy. But if we unpack the term, we can see an array of systems, organizations, and people:

- township clerk
- local water treatment systems
- 9-1-1 administrator
- traffic light engineer
- forest ranger
- state senate voting procedure
- infectious disease outbreak policies
- forest biological surveyor
- firefighter
- landfill engineer
- civil rights law
- county law enforcement officer
- interstate freshwater policy
- city librarian
- state labor union regulations
- accountants
- federal copyright office administrator
- graphic artist
- museum curator
- astronaut
- Navy SEAL

The point here is that using broad terms, like *the government*, in our writing can create vague statements. But if we open up such terms and look inside, we can see variety, difference, and probably a good deal of tension, which instantly makes thinking more rich, less finite, and less dull.

Good writers of all stripes find themselves unpacking terms. The process involves two important steps: (A) introducing the term itself and then (B) describing the details and differences lurking within that term. Both steps are apparent in the following sample passages:

Personal Narrative

There on the lakeshore with the sunset turning deep purple, my grandfather said what he'd told me the year before: "follow your dreams." This was his way of supporting me in whatever I plan to do. I understand his point and what it means about our relationship. But I also understand that my "dreams" aren't easy to follow. When I envision the future, I want a variety of things. I don't necessarily want fame or fortune, but I want to keep developing my skills in mathematics and music. And I want those skills to "pay off" somehow, to carry me into a successful adulthood. But at this point in my life, I can tell those different skills will run afoul of one another. During some weeks or months, I can barely manage to keep focus on one of my interests. Keeping both at the center of my life creates a constant challenge. So how can I follow both? How can I go where both might lead? I would need to cleave myself in two and watch the other half disappear. Given what I understand about college, internships, and the first years of professional life, I fear that my "dreams" will become enemies of one another. So while I value my grandfather's assertion, his devotion to me, I wonder if it would more realistic to say "manage your dreams."

Informative

While social media now shapes daily life for millions of people, it's difficult to make one reasonable point about it. **Social media**, *after all, includes a wide range of platforms that are used for many purposes. Facebook is home to older generations looking to share personal news and maintain connections to their past. LinkedIn serves professionals and students who hope to shape a career path. Instagram attracts young adults who are maintaining their network of friends and associates. Additionally, WhatsApp, Snapchat, YouTube, and X offer distinct functions that serve different audiences. It can even be said that each platform has its own character—in the same way different social clubs have their own mission and culture.*

Argumentative

A fashion influencer recently argued against "what society thinks" of an historic clothing trend, which begs the question: does society think? It's a *difficult question because **society** includes every school, church, farm, home, park, street, and alley. It also includes structures: sewers, pipes, lines, tunnels, dams, conduits, and all the tools for making and joining them. Society includes all demographics, generations, leaders, detractors, administrators, prisoners, officers, slackers, presidents, preachers, punks, activists, domestic terrorists, dogs, cats, and so on along with all the forms of communication that keep them connected. Finally, society includes the conceptual realm—theories, debates, and artistic expressions within its history. So can we imagine such a massive creature **thinking**? Sure. But any thought a society has would be filled with disagreement in the same way a comment section for a news article contains debate and contradiction. Can society think one thing about a clothing trend? Definitely not.*

Argumentative w/ Research

*Patriotism is not a single impulse to salute the flag and sing "The Star-Spangled Banner." In his influential book **Democracy in America**, Alexis de Tocqueville details two types of patriotism. First, he describes the emotional patriots, the people who are first to sing, to cheer, to rail against would-be enemies. However, he says, "there is another species of attachment to a country which is more rational than the one we have been describing. It is perhaps less generous and less ardent, but it is more fruitful and more lasting." Tocqueville goes on to describe a complex relationship between the individual citizen and the laws of a country—any systems that support the individual's desire to live a productive and full life.*

These passages show writers openly unpacking a term. In each case, the writer names the term (or phrase) and then shows multiple dimensions within that term. Often the writer even draws attention to the "complexity," "difference," or "contradictions" operating within the broad term. In essence, such passages slow readers down and prompt them to enter the world of broad terms—to open the door and see the many aspects operating inside.

Activity Prompt: In a small group, choose a broad term such as *technology* and then unpack it. Open it up. Rather than see it as a singular thing—with one set of effects and qualities—list as many qualities and effects as possible.

Seeking Complexity

Consider the good parts, the bad parts, and the ugly parts. And then discuss: How do all the differences affect your thinking about the broad term?

(2) Focusing the Questions

Nearly all writing projects have questions at their heart. Even if those questions are not stated directly, they drive the thinking, research, and even the nature of the project. Writers may begin with a broad question, but we benefit from *narrowing* it. In the same way professional divers straighten their bodies and slice into the water, writers get deeper into ideas by narrowing initial questions. Whether developing a thesis statement for an essay or trying to work further into an idea, writers who ask more focused questions will generate better, sharper thinking. Even in the middle of an essay, writers can pop a question. The narrower the question, the more powerfully it can function.

The first step is simply inspecting the nouns within the question and making them more specific. In the first list below, the questions are broad. In the second, the noun phrases are more precise:

Broad Questions

What behaviors make a winning team?
Why are big-box stores so successful?
How has feminism changed society?
How has computer technology changed society?

Narrower Questions

What forms of practice create more successful basketball teams?
What do successful football coaches do during halftime?
How does our Meijer store use local resources to increase sales?
How did feminism help change working conditions in the 1970s?
How have women pop stars influenced everyday conversations about gender?

How has AI technology impacted cell phone screen time?

Broad questions like those in the first list might provide some initial energy. But if they remain broad, the questions themselves can generate simplistic statements. Rather than probe the depths of an issue, a writer would be more likely to stay in the shallows. For example, imagine a writer taking the broad question about technology: *How has computer technology changed society?* It would be easy to list a huge range of changes—from the auto industry to politics, from social networking to classroom education. The list would go on and on. She wouldn't necessarily have to ask any probing questions. She wouldn't have to investigate, wonder, struggle to make connections, or think through specific concepts. She would simply make a huge list and be done thinking. But a more focused question would get her somewhere. For example, if she focused on robotic technology and its influence on physical human interaction, she could begin thinking about specific concepts. For instance, she could explore how robotic arms in assembly line manufacturing have impacted coworker relationships. Instead of listing a range of broad social changes, she would have to consider and research some specific forms of interaction: How do assembly-line coworkers share knowledge about the product? How do they signal uncertainty or concern about the product? How do they develop shared pride in the product?

A focused question, then, helps writers to go further—to pursue a line of thinking into deep water. And even after a project gains focus, we can keep pursuing the ideas. We can keep asking increasingly narrow questions. In fact, the best intellectual work often generates as many questions as it answers.

Personal Narrative

Broad: Why did I join band?
Narrow: Why did I choose to play drums in band when I had a fascination with trumpet?
Broad: How does school relate to music?
Narrow: How do my abilities in math support my attraction to percussion?
Broad: Why am I going away for college like most everyone else?
Narrow: Why am I leaving home to attend State when I can begin at a nearby two-year college?

Informative

Broad: What is the difference between Democrats and Republicans?

Narrow: How do Democrats and Republicans differ on legal immigration policy?

Broad: How does the government protect the environment?

Narrow: What are the current state laws on water pollution?

Broad: How much money does our school district spend?

Narrow: What portion of our school district's budget comes from local taxes?

Argumentative

Broad: Which political party is better on immigration?

Narrow: Which political party has a more comprehensive and accessible immigration policy?

Broad: What should we do about the environment?

Narrow: How can high school students influence state and local environmental policy?

Broad: Why should the local school levy pass?

Narrow: What services and programs would benefit from the latest school levy?

Activity Prompt: Narrow questions are more productive than broad questions. If you keep reshaping and honing them, the resulting questions perform a job: they help you to generate better, more sophisticated ideas. In a small group, take a topic like politics, air pollution, college tuition, or space travel. Generate a short list of broad questions about the topic. And then generate a short list of *more focused* questions. Discuss how the more focused questions impact your thinking. To answer them, what would you have to consider, research, or understand?

Key Questions

- For the main claim of your project, what nouns could be more specific?

- If you ask any questions—in your initial steps or in a draft—how can those questions be narrowed?

(3) Making New Comparisons

Humans are good at comparison. When we encounter a new idea or situation, our minds start reaching for familiar patterns so we can make sense of unfamiliar stimuli. When we get lost, we turn in all directions and try to get our mental hooks into something we recognize. The same thing happens when we come across an unfamiliar word: we try to find a familiar syllable or clump of letters. We grasp for meaning by grasping for things we already know. And we create new meaning by building on old intellectual ground. So in many respects, making comparisons is a basic operation. We do it naturally. But good writers also go looking for interesting comparisons. They try to see how one situation parallels another—how one theory, debate, or text shares qualities of another.

The easiest comparisons writers make are those between *similar* subjects. Consider, for example, two sports like NASCAR and Formula 1 racing. The connection is easy enough. Both sports are forms of contemporary auto racing. Similarities will be fairly obvious, the differences small. But let's broaden the scope. If we try to connect NASCAR and ancient Roman chariot races, we might discover more. Even though thousands of years (and the invention of gasoline engines) separate the two sports, they have some similarities. Comparing them may prompt some good thinking.

Comparing Racing Sports

In both sports, a crowd gathers around a circular track and watches while a few drivers risk life and limb to outpace competitors. There are no plays, quarters, half times, or breaks. It's unrelenting speed for as long as it takes. In both, the crowd can see the entire course of action, which is ongoing and constant, which means that anything can happen. The speed and force create ongoing energy and potential chaos—all completely within view. All strategies, dangers, and failures are immediately apparent. Any shortcomings or mistakes yield obvious, even disastrous, results. There is no time for the athletes or the onlookers to carefully plot out or chart the next move. In this sense, both NASCAR and chariot racing are true spectator sports. People crowd around the track and watch the spectacle. Maybe that simplicity speaks to the immense attraction and popularity through the ages.

Also consider what happens when a writer attempts a comparison that is even less obvious, for example, between NASCAR and moshing:

Comparing "Pit" Sports

How is a NASCAR event similar to moshing? At first glance, these two phenomena seem entirely different. Moshing is a form of aggressive dancing at hard rock or metal concerts. NASCAR is a spectator sport that involves highly trained professionals driving souped-up cars. But beneath the obvious contrasts, they share some qualities: Both NASCAR and moshing involve performance. Moshing takes place "in the pit" or the area directly in front of the stage. NASCAR events have an infield that hosts a range of notoriously rowdy behaviors. In this sense, moshing, and NASCAR share something. They involve collective public space. They both involve spectacle. And both run counter to mainstream official life. They are loud, raucous escapes from the world of responsibility. Moshers, in this respect, aren't all that different from avid NASCAR fans.

The point here is that insights come from making comparisons. When we bring together similar events or situations, we can see shared qualities and interesting trends with topics such as spectator sports through the centuries. And when we try to connect things that are *usually not associated*, we can generate even more interesting insights. We may even see a *pattern* of behavior—a rhythm or meaningful repetition that stretches across time and space. For example, consider how the NASCAR and moshing comparison can generate a compelling point:

Whether it's racetracks, mosh pits, conventional dance floors, or break dance cyphers, people flock to shared spaces where they not only watch but join the spectacle. There's something magnetic about the circle of activity, the competition at the center of things.

The writer here sees a subtle but grand pattern across different gatherings. These quiet similarities—those that aren't obvious or easy to see—reveal a deep connection among people. Good writers and thinkers explore the comparisons they make.

Activity Prompt: Good writers seek subtle patterns. They look for quiet but meaningful repetition. Consider a pattern in your school. For instance, how does classroom layout repeat from one room to another? Are the desks and tables organized in any particular fashion? Is the organization consistent? What reflex or ideas might be responsible for the layout? What does the repetition help you to understand about formal education?

Key Questions

Direct answers to the following questions (or any like them) don't always show up in completed writing, but they can certainly prompt sophisticated ideas:

- How are these situations related?
- Is some pattern at work?
- What's behind the pattern? (What force or reflex creates the particular rhythm or repetition? What does the repetition help us understand?)

(4) Creating Context

Imagine seeing a young man bouncing around in a room. He is tossing his head around, throwing his arms in the air, and occasionally jumping up and down. If we were trying to figure him out—what the heck he's doing—we might conclude that he's terribly sick or turning into a zombie. But then imagine someone hitting a switch and turning the room into a concert hall. Suddenly, we hear the music and see a crowd of people around him doing the same thing. It becomes clear: the young man is in a mosh pit with hundreds of others. We now understand the *context*, the activity around him, and so we better understand the meaning of his actions. We could get an even better understanding if we broaden our perspective further. We might, for instance, read about the history of moshing—when it became popular, the type of music associated with it, the lyrics and messages of that musical style. We could read about the broader cultural trends that first prompted adolescent men to start bashing into others as a form of physical communion. We might discover something about the quiet loneliness that plagues suburban teenagers or the need for some kind of physical intensity in a culture dominated by physical comfort. Whatever we discover, that broader context would help us to see layers of meaning in the young man's movements.

Without context, people's dance moves—or people in general—don't make much sense. The same goes for reports, essays, articles, books, and even pieces of art. If we don't understand the surrounding activity, we likely won't understand the thing itself. We should, then, examine the time and place that gave rise to the issue, the event, the behavior, or the text. Even the most abstract ideas have origins. And writers try to understand those origins. They try to see how the tensions and trends of the day relate to the thing they are studying. Here's the difficult part: those trends and tensions aren't always obvious. This means we get to frame things for ourselves. We get to make decisions about the surrounding factors—which are most important, which help us to understand the specific topic? Which are least important?

All writers have to determine where to begin thinking, where to focus, what to include in their examination, and what to exclude. Imagine, for instance, that we want to write about the American singer Bob Dylan. We could start creating context in any number of ways—depending on the factors we find most influential:

A. Other Songwriters: The 1960s in America were defined by civic unrest. Artists from every genre gave voice and imagery to the collective sentiments against power and corruption. Along with artists such as Woody Guthrie, Joan Baez, and John Lennon, Bob Dylan gave this volatile era a permanent place in American history.

B. Other Literary Figures: The voice of Bob Dylan emerges from the middle of the twentieth century—in a decade heavily influenced by Beat poets such as William S. Burroughs, Jack Kerouac, and Allan Ginsberg.

C. Social Issues: After WWII, America was settling into suburban life. But along came the rebellious 1960s and with them, the voice of Bob Dylan.

Each statement creates context but establishes a slightly different framework for understanding Dylan's work: Statement A puts Dylan in a scene with other songwriters who often wrote about political and cultural issues. Statement B draws attention to Dylan's artistic qualities. Statement C establishes a broad cultural tension between quiet suburban life and the upheavals of the 1960s.

Contextualizing statements are powerful, especially at the start of a writing project. They can control how we read or think about people, texts, or events.

When someone says, "Look at that sunset!" most of us will turn our heads and look to the sky rather than the grass. The same thing happens with contextualizing statements. If we begin an examination of Bob Dylan with a statement about Post-War suburbia, then we have established a way of thinking—one that is different from other contextualizing statements.

When writers create context, they determine for themselves, and anyone reading or listening, the most important issues and weighty details. They also determine the insignificant: ideas, people, and issues that won't be examined. Creating context is like drawing boundaries and distinguishing between what matters and what doesn't. It involves some personal decisions and creativity. In other words, context is something that every writer can *create*. One writer may define the situation one way. The next may define it another. As a later chapter explains, writers also should try to understand the context of any text or written argument they want to analyze. That process is slightly different, but both moves (creating and understanding context) are powerful ways to shape the writing project.

Activity Prompts: (1) Decide what cultural, political, or religious factors give way to rap music. What attitudes created the audience for rap? (2) If you were examining a particular rap artist, how would you create context for readers? What cultural or political factors would you mention? What factors would be most critical for establishing a framework? (3) In a small group, consider the songwriter Taylor Swift. Write three short contextual passages (like those for Dylan above): (A) Other Songwriters, (B) Other Women in Pop Culture, (C) Social Issues.

Key Questions

- What are the important factors in understanding the topic?
- Are those factors related to social, political, or natural events?
- How did those factors impact the topic?

(5) Advanced Move: Denying the Usual Associations

Ideas don't exist in isolation. They hang around with several other ideas that have become associated with them. We see them together. If one idea is around, its associates are usually not far behind. For instance, consider a mosquito. When most people imagine a mosquito—the *idea* of a mosquito—they also picture itching, blood, a swollen mark on the arm, and maybe a can of repellent. And for millions of people throughout the world, the idea of a mosquito comes along with a fear of malaria. In other words, it's almost impossible to think of a *mosquito* without thinking of these other things. The idea has a *string of associations* that goes zooming through our brains.

Or consider *high school*. The idea comes along with teachers, books, hallways, organized sports, and maybe marching band. When someone says anything about *high school*, we probably don't think of outer space or antelopes running over a desert plain. Why? Because language is *associative*: it makes connections for us. And the most obvious associations are not random or even personal. (Granted, everyone has personal associations and memories that come rolling along with particular words. When we think *high school*, we likely think of particular people, rooms, and events. But language works because so many of our associations are shared. We can communicate because we're *not* all quietly generating our own personal associations with each word. If we were, it'd be as though every single person were speaking a foreign language. We'd need dictionaries and translators for every statement.)

The associative power of language operates in any topic or widely debated issue. For instance, consider arguments related to *privacy*, a term that brings along others: *individual, personal information, inalienable rights, search and seizure*. These concepts come on the coattails of *privacy* and vice versa. They are clustered together in common thinking. They are like a small gang of concepts that consistently show up to the (intellectual) party. Of course, that's not all bad. In fact, academic disciplines themselves depend on associative power. If one is studying political science, it's good to learn the above associations. Understanding the relationships between privacy and its band of others is part of being a political science student. One cannot unlearn them and shouldn't necessarily try. The associations, in other words, are valuable. They make thinking happen. Once *privacy* comes up, political scientists immediately understand the surrounding issues, the potential questions, and the intellectual tangles. They know, for instance, that *privacy* involves some belief in an individual's right to make personal decisions: where to live, how to worship, how not to worship, whom to marry, and so on. People who don't know these associations would have a difficult time. They'd flounder to understand even the beginnings of an article or lecture.

Although common associations are important, they can also act like blinders. They can keep writers from seeing other possible connections. And so sophisticated writing *sometimes* denies usual associations. It's a daring but powerful move. It shows that writers can think (and even thrive) *without the usual intellectual associations*. Whenever we split up those conceptual clusters, exploratory thinking can begin.

As with other moves in this chapter, denying a usual association can often happen in a single paragraph. While approaches vary, denying a usual association involves two important steps: (1) The writer spends time with *usual* pairings—the two or three words that typically operate together. (2) The writer then explains how separating the ideas impacts their meaning or how one of the terms changes without its usual pairing.

Personal Narrative

When people think about debates, they may imagine two opponents who both speak exceptionally well—who can fire off lots of points quickly. In other words, people couple debate and public speaking. But I'm here to say the opposite. As a successful debate team member, I am nothing close to eloquent. I don't speak well in public, especially under pressure. In fact, I'm bad at finishing sentences, unless, of course, I'm writing them down. My nerves get the best of me. The quiet conversation in my own head somehow shuts down my own mouth. It's frustrating. However, my nerves do not work against me as a debate team member. In fact, the intensity of competition even charges up my ability to recall important information and link it to the issue. When a debate moderator poses a question, my mind instantly goes to work, and I find myself charting out the most logical and forceful points for the team. In this sense, I'm a crucial debate team member and, as it turns out, a great debater.

Informative

When we talk about privacy in America, we often think of the individual. Privacy, we assume, is an individual phenomenon. However, most often, privacy is not about an individual, at least not completely. Very little, if anything, about human life is truly closed off from others. Our lives are shared with spouses, siblings, doctors, ministers, parents, friends, coworkers. If anything, we have a long list of daily collaborators—people who know things about us, who keep those things relatively, but not completely, quiet. More accurately, privacy is a behavior pattern that allows us to choose who gets to know certain things about us. Privacy does involve choice—the decision to determine who knows what. When that decision gets taken away, or blurred in some fashion, our privacy gets compromised. In this sense, maybe privacy is not a closet where we keep secrets, but a web that we manage. If privacy is a web, then invasion of privacy is both easier to detect and harder to manage. And if this is true, it raises many questions about credit cards, corporate control of personal information, hacking, online dating, and so on.

Argumentative

Screen time has unofficially been linked to social media. Parents and teachers constantly urge students to "limit their screen time." The cautions about and rules against too much screen time assume screens always, or most often, involve social media. The automatic belief is that students with their faces in phones or laptops are probably committing the sins of Tik Tock, Instagram, whichever platform is trending. But screen time also involves reading, researching, or browsing the billion (plus) available websites populating the internet. Screen time means finding out about Shakespeare, biology, political party platforms, local laws, sports schedules, lunch menus—in other words, nearly everything related to scholastic and daily life.

More importantly, screen time is crucial for professional and academic success. Imagine someone telling a CEO, teacher, or school superintendent to limit their screen time. Imagine telling a corporate CFO to limit how much they spend investigating data on competing companies—all of which would likely come via computer screen. Imagine telling a librarian to spend less time investigating the available books and periodicals, all of which come in electronic catalogues. Such cautions would undermine the very nature of their work. Screen time is, in this era and certainly going forward into the future, necessary for work. It is not exclusively, or even often, about social media.

Activity Prompt: Choose a term that consistently shows up in class reading or discussion and consider its usual associations—the other ideas that you *instantly think of when you see or hear the term*. In a group, discuss how those associative terms impact or even direct your thinking. What debates, positions, or events come to mind? What beliefs come to mind?

Writing Prompts

Writing for complexity means cracking open our own thinking. The mission is to make our thinking less finite, less predictable, and less dull—to go looking for layers that we'd otherwise miss:

1. Consider a common idea that seems simple, one-dimensional, and obvious—for example, friendship, kindness, desire, or hope. Seek complexity in that idea. Apply the moves from this chapter: ask focused questions, unpack terms, make connections, and deny the usual associations. Develop a brief essay that reveals layers of your topic. After you've developed a draft, go back through and unpack further. Add full paragraphs that crack open your own broad terms and deny the associations that you relied on.

2. Think about your situation: In addition to being a student, maybe you work part-time. Maybe you're an athlete or musician. Maybe you're deeply involved in politics or a church group. Whatever your situation, how are you part of a pattern? Write a brief essay that explains your experience as a particular type of student. Consider the moves for seeking complexity: unpack broad terms, ask focused questions, make connections, and deny the usual associations.

3. Take on a common idea in education, such as *knowledge, science, instruction, culture, memory*, or *technology*. Use the steps for seeking complexity to flesh out nuances that otherwise gets ignored or missed. Try to deny the common associations. Explain how the usual clusters of thought stop thinking. Ask focused questions. And unpack broad terms that might conceal dimensions of the concept. What insights emerge? Why is this new way of thinking important?

2 Applying a Concept

A concept is an idea that moves through time, across situations, from one person to another. Concepts are part of the world. They determine how we live, what we do, and, of course, how we think. And in scholastic life, concepts rule. They drive the daily work, long-term studies, experiments, and written scholarship. Every discipline functions on some basic and not-so-basic concepts. Psychology includes self, id, ego, memory, adaptation, decompensation, abnormality, extrinsic motivation, and so on. Physics includes force, mass, acceleration, motion, velocity, and time. Such concepts are the basic ingredients of study. Without them, thinking and writing would cease. There'd be no new experiments, no new hypotheses, no new theories, no new ideas, nothing.

Students can harness the power of concepts when they apply them to specific texts, cases, or situations. And that is the focus of this chapter: how to apply a general concept to something specific. This doesn't mean physical application but an intellectual process that involves choosing a concept, adopting language about the concept, and applying that language to a specific text or situation. This chapter will also help students move from identification to application, an essential step in developing more sophisticated writing. In other words, students may be able to identify an element but struggle to write about it. For instance, they may be able to call out the *protagonist* of a story but wonder what can be said about that protagonist. This chapter can help students see concepts as engines—propulsion systems for new ideas. It offers three moves: (1) adopting specific language, (2) taking on big concepts, (3) transporting concepts.

(1) Adopting Specific Language

When we apply a concept, we need some specific language, even a formal definition, which can then help us generate ideas. For example, consider the *protagonist*, the main character of a story. It's often easy to identify or label the protagonist of a story, but when we apply the concept, we can discover something about that protagonist. Because we need specific language, let's borrow a definition from the English department at the University of Victoria:

> *The protagonist in a work of fiction is the character with whom the reader is meant to be chiefly concerned; she or he is the main character, who, whether sympathetic or not, is the focus of the plot. A work of narrative or drama may have more than one protagonist.*

With such a definition, we can apply language to *anything* with a protagonist: a film, television show, play, short story, or a popular literary work such as J. R. R. Tolkien's *Lord of the Rings*. Notice how the following passage explains different ways in which we are "chiefly concerned" with Tolkien's protagonist, Frodo Baggins. In other words, the following doesn't simply say that Frodo *is* the protagonist because we are chiefly concerned with him. Instead, it explains *how* we are concerned:

> *We care about Frodo and his mission. We follow him from the moment he inherits the ring of power, so we watch him go from an innocent bystander to an active player in the battle for Middle Earth. Of course, we hope that Frodo and his companion, Sam, survive—that they don't end up as spider food or Orc victims—but we also hope that Frodo does not give in to the ring. We want him to survive, save the world, and not crave power. We want him to stay uncorrupted, and this is our most consistent but quiet concern throughout the story.*

Even by explaining how we are "chiefly concerned" about this protagonist, the passage is now applying the concept. But we could go even further by applying the concept to specific scenes or actions. The following passage does the same as the first: it applies the general concept (protagonist) to the specific character (Frodo), but it focuses on a specific scene:

> *At the climax of the final book, just as Frodo prepares to destroy the ring by throwing it into the fires of Mt. Doom, he hesitates. He decides he will keep it. "It is precious to me," he says. Our concern now has reached its peak. We realize, after hundreds of pages and many scenes following Frodo through hardship, that he is falling prey to the ring. His selflessness has withered away. We fear that Middle Earth and all of the characters that have come to matter to us will be destroyed because Frodo has, in the end, given in to greed.*

Notice that we're not simply describing the character. Instead, we're *applying a concept* that allows us to think about Frodo in a particular way—how, and for what reasons, a reader cares about Frodo. If the definition we had chosen to apply focused on the protagonist's relationships to other characters or how a protagonist relates to the setting, then the above passages would have followed a different path.

What's important here is that new thinking happens—almost instantaneously—when a concept gets applied to a specific situation or text. The general (concept) interacts with the particulars (scenes), and ideas begin to form. After the initial thinking gets underway, we could tread onward and examine smaller passages, scenes, or dimensions. Notice, also, how the passage uses the definition of protagonist. It gives a direct quotation from a reliable source as part of the initial explanation, relies on a key phrase from that quotation ("chiefly concerned"), and then *comes back around* to that language to further develop ideas. In other words, it shows how we can return to key phrases and use them to continue writing. And this move works not only for literary studies. Writers can apply *any* concept to *any* situation.

Activity Prompt for Literary Study: In a small group, focus on a literary element such as *protagonist, antagonist, setting, climax,* or *conflict*. Refer to a formal definition—one provided by your teacher or an online source. Apply specific language from that definition to a story, novel, or film, and discuss how the particulars fit the definition itself. As your discussion continues, examine specific scenes or passages and try to discover how those specifics support the definition.

Activity Prompt for Expository or Argumentative Writing: In a small group, focus on a widely shared concept such as *freedom, patriotism, social justice, religious freedom, free market capitalism,* or *corporate responsibility*. Find a definition online. Apply language from that definition to a specific situation and discuss how the particulars fit the definition itself. As your discussion continues, explain how specifics within the situation support the definition.

(2) Taking on the Big Concepts

In the original *Jaws* movie (way back in 1975), three men set out to find and destroy a notorious great white shark. On a tiny fishing vessel, they make their way into open water. They are emboldened, in good cheer, and ready for victory. As one character, Martin Brody, is throwing bait off the back of the boat, he encounters the shark for the first time. As the huge animal surfaces, Brody sees with his own eyes the trouble ahead of them. His face goes flat. He realizes that they are outmatched. The shark is simply too big, the situation too intense for the tools available. He backs slowly into the cabin and tells the captain, "You're gonna need a bigger boat." The same goes for thinking and writing. As we go along through school, we encounter increasingly complex situations and texts, so we need bigger concepts to deal with them. In short, we need bigger boats.

All students and scholars must deal with increasingly bigger concepts. Consider, for example, how science courses evolve as we go through school. Early on, we learn some basic concepts: friction, mass, speed, and so on. We watch balls rolling down planes and balloons bursting. Then, we learn about gases, liquids, and solids. In the next course, we study the interaction of elements—the formation of compounds, the intermingling of atomic parts. If we go all the way to physics, we start learning about the movement and patterns of atomic parts. As with all academic fields, the further we go, the more complex concepts we encounter. Complex concepts require more explanation than simple concepts. Consider the following examples:

- Simple Concepts: conflict, character, protagonist, freedom, technology, cost, force
- Complex Concepts: existentialism, antihero, cyborgism, cost/benefit ratio, thermodynamics, particulate radiation

So what does this all mean for writing? It means writers grappling with complex concepts must *slow down*. Before we can begin applying a complex concept, we must make sense of it—to explain it to ourselves and others. For that reason, sophisticated writers often take a full paragraph (or several) to flesh out a concept. For example, the following passage explains *antihero*, a complex literary concept, one that needs more than a simple definition. The passage illustrates two key strategies: First, it explains exactly how the concept is more complex than its more basic counterpart. In other words, it describes what makes the idea worth a close look! Second, the passage uses a brief comparison to help characterize the nature of the concept:

*Often, it seems, protagonists in mainstream works are more **antihero** than hero. Antiheroes populate movies, comic books, videos, and literary works. What are antiheros? Are they simply the opposite of conventional heroes? Several sources explain antiheroes as characters who lack conventional virtues such as courage, strength, moralism, or selflessness. Antiheroes may even be cowardly, weak, dishonest, or selfish. They are problems to themselves. They are sometimes their own worst enemy.*

    Even with bad traits, antiheroes remain the chief concern of a story. Audiences want them to succeed, to overcome their questionable traits or win despite them. In fact, antiheroes are sometimes more loved than conventional heroes—more interesting to readers and viewers, more memorable for some reason. Like a refined dessert, they are both sweet and sour. They contain conflicting flavors, qualities that usually compete with one another. This means the antihero is part of a story's conflict, sometimes the main conflict. In traditional stories with traditional heroes, the conflict lies outside of the main characters. But if an antihero is involved, then conflict and character become married or at least joined in some fashion, and this makes the story more interesting. As Tayler Swift sang, "It must be exhausting always rooting for the antihero," but it may also be quite entertaining.

The above passages use some common sentence strategies that can be applied widely. Notice some key opening phrases that help writers to dig further into their thinking:

- In other words...
- But even with such...
- This means...
- Like a...

Activity Prompt: In a discussion group, take on a complex concept such as *environmental justice*. Look it up online and consult at least two different sources. Then, try to draft a paragraph that thoroughly explains what environmental justice is, c, and why it matters to some people more than others. In your paragraph, offer a helpful comparison—a metaphor or simile that draws attention to important aspects of the concept.

(3) Advanced Move: Transporting a Concept

Concepts are portable. They get carried over mountains, across oceans, and through time. Democracy, for example, was transported from ancient Greece to sixteenth-century England and then to the American colonies. As settlers moved west across the Great Plains and over the Rocky Mountains, they carried along their concepts of private land, squatters' rights, statehood, and individual wealth.

Transporting concepts is common work in scholarly life. Psychology borrows from sociology. Literary studies borrow from philosophy. Education borrows from psychology. Engineering borrows from physics. Business borrows from everyone and anyone. And to repeat a point made above, concepts are *generative*. They make thinking and writing happen. So borrowing concepts from another discipline or field of study means borrowing *a way of thinking*. Imported concepts can solve old problems and create new insights. Velcro, rock and roll, electricity, even the World Wide Web all came along because people borrowed concepts from one field and applied them to another. And here's the interesting point for our concerns: transporting even relatively simple concepts can make sophisticated writing. For example, the following passage takes a well-established idea in physics and applies it to sports. The concept adds a notch more sophistication to a basic idea about seasonal momentum in organized athletics:

> *The laws of physics say an object in motion tends to stay in motion unless another object or some external force interferes. In other words, if an object is rushing forward at a given speed, it continues unless something works against it. The same can be said about athletic teams. Each game, meet, or competition creates a collective energy, momentum that carries the team forward in the days after. That energy is then met with the next external force—the next competition or even the next practice. Will the next opposing team disrupt the established momentum? Will the next practice bring out the team's strongest impulses or show its vulnerabilities? The best teams see themselves in this light. Rather than focusing on each individual game or match, they understand themselves as a single entity moving forward through the season.*

This kind of conceptual blending happens constantly. Sometimes, writers adopt concepts from across the hall or around the corner to see how they can refresh their daily work. But the process also happens quietly, even unconsciously.

Sometimes, writers don't even realize what they are doing. The foreign concept hitches a ride and shows up in their thoughts. Regardless of how it happens—intentionally or accidentally—the process of transporting a concept cultivates sophisticated writing. Ideas that may never meet are suddenly sharing mental space. And when that happens, two intellectual traditions converge. All the assumptions, terminology, and research methods start interacting.

Imagine a student who's well-versed in music, one who's taken an initial course in theory. The following passage borrows a concept from music theory and transports it to an argument about school policy. This longer example relies on three basic steps, each operating in its own paragraph: (1) Describe the concept in the simplest terms possible. In other words, the first paragraph attempts to make the concept clear to non-specialized readers, to people outside of music theory. (2) Explain how the concept sheds light on something outside its original discipline or field of study. (3) Apply the point in step two to a specific situation or condition. All three paragraphs, then, work to transport the concept:

> *In music theory, melody refers to the movement of individual notes through time. The familiar lines we all hum when we think of our favorite pop songs are melodies. Melody isn't just a free-for-all. There are certain conventions, or sonic patterns, that govern how melodies work, and those conventions are largely set by the key signature—the broader chordal atmosphere in which a melody lives. For instance, if we're in the key of A, a D is the fourth note and wants to resolve to the third note of the scale or C#. The listener wants that resolution. Until the note resolves, there's sonic tension or anticipation. Listeners wait for the fourth note to slide gracefully down to its proper (regular) place in the chord. When it happens and the end of some phrase, listeners feel gratified—as though our mini-audio journey has ended.*
>
> *People are not so different from notes. We live according to conventions and even the structural atmosphere around us. How we function—how we sound—is a function of that atmosphere. We don't want to remain in tension for very long. We want to slide into our chordal place, to line up according to the tonality of the surrounding atmosphere. In fact, it's stressful on the body and mind to be out of place for very long. When we're at school, we quickly learn the structural norms. We learn how to go about moving from hour to hour, day to day. In other words, school has a key signature, and that signature establishes tendencies. Certain behaviors ring easily and pleasantly. Others create tension.*

> Last week, when hundreds of students protested recent budget cuts to athletic and music programs, they were stepping out of class and out of their conventional place. It wasn't natural or pleasing. Nobody wanted to leave their role. Contrary to what one administrator suggested, students are not "always looking for a reason to stir up trouble." If that were the case, there would be nonstop protests. Instead, most of us want to thrive in the given structure, but if the structure itself is threatened—if big programs get cut—then some, even many, feel obligated to sound off, to make unpleasant noise, not for long but long enough to get noticed.

As this passage illustrates, writers can explore other disciplines outside of language arts or English. Something we read in psychology, music, sociology, history, science, or mathematics can be imported to our writing goals.

Activity Prompt: In a small group, list several concepts central to a course you are taking. Choose one of those concepts and discuss how it could be applied to a current topic. How would you describe the concept to others not familiar with your field? What insights would come from transporting the concept to another discipline? Imagine, for instance, that you're writing about video game violence. How might the *id*, a psychological concept, shed light on the attraction to certain games? Or how might *ethnocentrism*, a concept from sociology, help you understand typical video game characters?

Writing Prompts

Sophisticated writing often happens when concepts are applied to specific situations or texts. Insights develop when writers examine the general idea interacting with specifics. The following project prompts could generate brief essays (of several well-developed paragraphs) or even lengthy research essays:

1. Personal/Expository: Consider one of the following complex concepts: existential angst, antihero, postmodern dislocation, or cyborgism. Consult a variety of sources to find out how experts define the phrase. Apply language from one of those sources to a specific habit, pattern, or decision in your life. How does the concept help you understand your behavior?
2. Expository: Apply a concept you chose for option 1 to a fictional character—to someone in film or literature. Remember to narrow

in on specific scenes and events. Apply the concept to specific decisions, actions, and even emotions.

3. Personal/Expository: Take a common concept from this book and apply it to a situation in your daily life. At first, you might wonder how these concepts (such as complexity, subtle tension, dualistic thinking) relate at all to your life. But try borrowing specific language. For example, consider the following passage from Chapter 6:

> *Dualities can bully our brains. They can gather in our thoughts and make us imagine two, and only two, contrary possibilities. In short, they can create* **dualistic thinking**—*an inability to see gray areas.*

How might an "inability to see gray areas" work in your life? How does this language help to make sense of a specific decision that you had to make?

4. Expository: Examine a scientific concept (particulate radiation, gravitational pull, molecular diffusion) or a legal concept (fraud, material witness, habeas corpus). Consult a variety of sources until you think you understand the concept. And then apply the concept to an artistic or literary work. Remember to use specific terminology and come back around to specific phrases as you apply the concept.

3 Analyzing Arguments

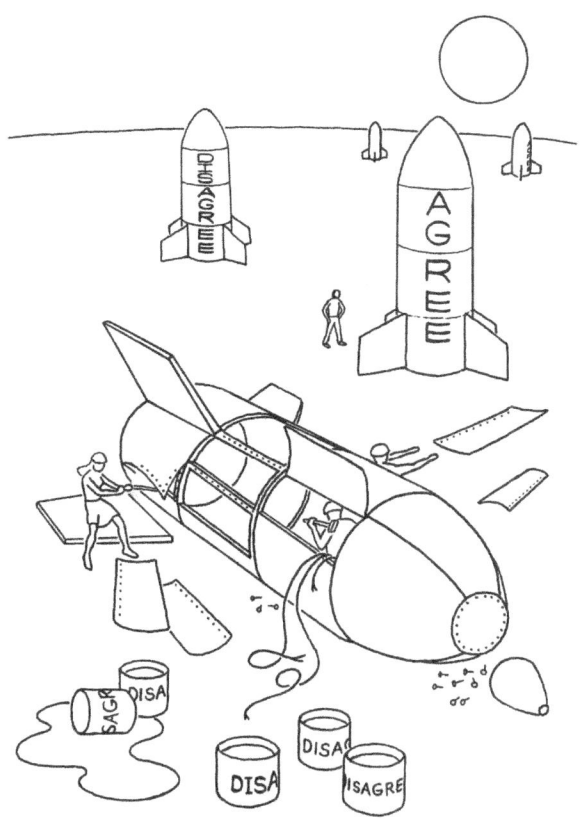

Argumentation is a prevailing force in popular culture. All major news outlets feature pundits who make fierce—often terrifying—claims about the country. Internet influencers perform their judgments on products, services, and other people. Pop stars, rappers, and celebrities of every stripe take strident positions on everything from food to politics. In other words, students grow up in an agonistic culture, one steeped in formal and informal argumentation. And from the time they begin writing in school, they are prompted to develop argumentative essays. In fact, as I observed after twenty-five years of teaching, incoming college students often associate the act of writing with the act of argument. They find it difficult to analyze without asserting overt judgment.

In some respects, the educational focus on argumentation makes sense. After all, arguments shape lives. They start countries. They get people thrown in jail and freed from tyranny. And in academic life, arguments make disciplines come alive. Much work published in academia is argumentative in nature. Scholars at all levels and in all fields study one another's arguments—their assertions about what's true, what's false, what should be funded, ignored, or emphasized in further study. It's easy to see why argumentation became central to writing instruction through the twentieth century. (Most college students still write research argument essays as the final step in first-year composition courses.) However, in recent decades, analysis has become a persistent and important part of writing curricula. Most first-year college courses also include argument analysis as a precursor to argumentation itself. High school and college teachers alike see the value of promoting rigorous analytical impulses. The rationale is easy to detect: If students lack sophisticated analytical skills, they may not grasp the nuances of others' opinions. They may misread, misinterpret, and misjudge the value of an argument. They may enter the world of argumentation and struggle to gain traction.

With guidance, even the most tentative writers can analyze an argument. In fact, developing writers often appreciate the palpable and widely applicable steps of argument analysis. If they follow some conventions, they can quickly generate compelling insights about someone else's argument. This empowers young writers and gives them increased agility when it comes to writing their own arguments.

This chapter focuses exclusively on analysis: taking an argument apart, examining its elements, and explaining how they function. It offers a model for helping students understand key elements. While later chapters examine acts of making arguments, this chapter isolates the move of dismantling—of carefully taking apart and inspecting what has been asserted. To that end, the chapter focuses on the following strategies: (1) considering the context, (2) analyzing the reasoning, (3) analyzing the writer/speaker, (4) identifying counterarguments, concessions, and qualifiers, (5) analyzing the audience, (6) calling out unstated reasons, (7) calling out the quiet argument.

At the outset, it's important to clarify some basic terms, those that students will likely encounter as they learn about argumentative writing and argument analysis. While lengthier explanations are given throughout the chapter, the following definitions may help students from the start:

- Claim: an arguable assertion made about a topic. An argument's main claim can also be called a thesis.
- Position: often interchangeable with "main claim," a writer/speaker's position is simply the opinion put forward in the argument.
- Context: the surrounding cultural atmosphere of an argument. This includes attitudes, beliefs, and overt political debates that have shaped a topic.
- Reasoning: the basic rational steps leading to an argumentative claim.
- Evidence: any information that reinforces the argumentative reasoning. Evidence includes facts, statistics, data, and testimony.
- Counterargument: language that challenges or refutes an opposing position.
- Concession: language that acknowledges the value or worth of an opposing position.
- Qualifier: language that limits the scope of the writer/speaker's argument.

(1) Considering the Context

First, analyzing an argument requires an understanding of *context*: the situation surrounding the argument itself. In simple terms, this means finding when and where the argument was written or made public. If we get a sense of cultural surroundings (shared concerns and attitudes of the era), we can better determine the role of other elements. For instance, if we are examining the Declaration of Independence, we should try to understand something about the late eighteenth century. Back then, royalty was a widely accepted idea. Most people in Europe and the American colonies believed in the power of some unelected people over the masses. Equality between a royal person and a nonroyal person was a radical idea. If we know that about the context, we will read the Declaration in a particular light. We'll better understand its urgency. (For more on the Declaration and its context, see Chapter 1.)

The same goes for any topic in any era. Widely shared attitudes and beliefs help to shape what gets said, what gets left unstated, and what must be argued with intensity. For example, if we were examining an argument on student loans in twenty-first-century America, we would do well to understand some trends: that most high school students plan to attend college, that college is costly, that most American families need financial assistance paying for college, that most students leave college with significant debt, that tuition shows no signs of coming down in the future. Understanding such trends would help us analyze any given argument about loans. We would know from the start why the subject mattered to people, why arguments were being made, and who cared.

Examining context requires some research, and a little browsing goes a long way. One key strategy is to browse contemporary articles from newspapers, monthly magazines, or blogs. We can learn a good deal about public opinion from reading titles and summaries because they tap into day-to-day events and people's responses to them. In short, armed with a good search engine, it's not difficult to get a sense of the social attitudes about a given issue. If we are looking into student loans, we could enter any of the following phrases:

- student loans
- student loans news
- student loans opinion
- student loans top stories
- student loans debate

Spending an hour (or a class session) in context mode helps us to sense the common opinions related to the topic in question. (Ancient Greek teachers referred to this process as *surveying the doxa*. It was considered the first step in generating an argument. The next chapter will further examine this process.) This step can also help to generate an introductory passage—whether writing an analysis or an argument.

Activity Prompt: In a small group, choose a topic such as cyberbullying, music subscription services, the current voting age, diversity, and Hollywood. Using several different search engines, enter the topic phrase along with words such as *opinion, debate, top stories*. After browsing at least five articles or pages, write a brief passage that describes cultural attitudes toward your chosen topic.

Key Questions

After browsing some online sources related to the topic, consider the following:

- What are the widely expressed opinions about the topic?
- What do people disagree about?
- Why do people argue about the topic?
- How does the target text (the argument under consideration) relate to others' positions?

(2) Analyzing the Reasoning

Reasoning is a huge can of intellectual worms. Entire academic departments and countless books focus solely on argumentative reasoning. But it needn't be overwhelming. It can come down to two primary elements: Arguments depend on a *claim* (an assertion that expresses someone's position) and *reasoning* (the *why* or justification for someone's claim). These two elements make arguments go. For example, let's return to the topic of student loans. Of course, any number of claims can be made about the topic, but consider the simple claim that *loans should be interest-free*. In the following passage, the reasoning builds to and supports that claim:

> Most students today simply cannot pay for college, nor can their parents. In fact, paying for a full four-year degree is now far beyond the ability of nearly all American families. Only the very wealthy can pay for an entire college education, which means nearly all college students graduate with some form of debt, which stretches into decades or over lifetimes. Because a generation of debtors is bad for the overall economy, student loans should, at the least, be interest-free.

As with many written arguments, the reasons in this passage are packed together with the claim. But if we were to list them out, the elements might look like this:

Claim: Student loans should be interest-free.

Reasons:

> Most college students cannot pay for college and, therefore, must get loans.
>
> Most college students will graduate with major loan debt.
>
> A majority of college students shouldn't graduate with growing debt.
>
> A generation of debtors is bad for the economy.

Analyzing an argument requires that we pull apart the reasons—that we detect and untangle each reason from others. Most arguers don't call out their reasons directly. They rarely list them! Instead, they weave their reasons together with personal testimony, facts, and information from sources, which means the reasons might be separated by many paragraphs or pages. So when we're analyzing, we have to look for statements that justify the main claim by asking *why* (and *why else*) the writer/speaker holds that particular position.

Key Questions

After carefully reading the argument, ask the following:

- Why does the writer/speaker hold that particular position?
- What reasons are given?
- What reasons are suggested but not necessarily stated?

(3) Analyzing the Writer/Speaker

When we analyze speakers and writers, we examine the way they figure into their arguments. This is a relatively easy task when writers talk openly about themselves. When they mention their own experiences or offer personal reflections, they make clear how they figure into the argument. When writers don't draw attention to themselves, we must work a little harder. We must determine something about writers based on *how they've presented their argument*. For example, consider the following two passages. While the first writer draws attention to himself, the second does not, but both writers can be analyzed:

Matthew: I am a college student, a single father, and a part-time salesperson. I have two loans from two different lending institutions. I'll likely graduate with more than $20,000 of debt. I'll immediately start looking for a job in my field and hopefully start climbing out of this financial hole. If I'm lucky enough to get a job, I'll cling to it and hope that I can get out of the red within a decade, but I know I might pay on that debt for the rest of my life.

Kelli: Student loan debt is crushing an entire generation. It's not only the staggering totals that loom after graduation but the interest that keeps those totals bearing down for years to come. Millions of college students enter the workforce indebted and beaten down before they can even imagine participating in the American dream.

It's not difficult to detect Matthew. He's fully present in the passage. His personal experiences connect him to the topic and establish his authority to make claims about student loans. On the other hand, Kelli does not draw attention to her own experiences. We might, then, wonder about her connection to the issue. But we don't necessarily need her personal story. We can, instead, inspect her words and sentences. For instance, notice Kelli's use of *crushing, staggering, loom,* and *bearing down*. These terms tell us something about her relationship to the topic. We know she sees the topic from a student's perspective. We also know, from the last sentence of her passage, that she has a broad understanding of the issue. "Millions of college students," she tells us, are currently faced with the problem. If we were to keep reading Kelli's argument, we would look for more clues about her relationship to the issue.

Analyzing a writer or speaker, then, is a process of tracing words and phrases that tell us something about the persona or *ethos*. Each word choice, each sentence, and each point can shed some light—not simply where the writer stands but what they value, what they assume in relation to the topic at hand. However, we should be careful. If we're not attentive to our own reading, we might be inclined to conjure biases about the writer. This can take an ugly turn if we allow those suspicions to steer our thinking. We might characterize the writer in the worst possible terms:

- "Adam Hollings just wants to come off smarter than everyone else."
- "Clara Knightly is just knocking everyone who disagrees with her."

The same can happen in the opposite direction. We might allow our biases to steer us toward the most glowing understanding of a writer:

- "He has everyone's best interests in mind."
- "They have a full understanding of the culture and their audience."

Such statements often say more about the analyst than the writer or speaker in question. Also, they leave behind analysis and get into evaluation. In other words, such statements condemn or celebrate the writer. Instead, we should stay committed to analysis—explaining the function of the elements.

A Close Look at Purpose

Understanding an argument depends largely on understanding the *purpose*—or the motivating drive—of the argument. Is the writer out to condemn something, to fix a shared way of thinking, or to propose a new way of thinking? While there are many purposes, the following general types show up regularly in argumentative texts:

- Supporting or Condemning (*This Is or Isn't a Good Idea*): In this type of project, writers support or condemn a specific practice, idea, or policy. They argue, for example, that some new research misses the mark, that conventional logic is sound, or that a new perspective is worth close attention. In such arguments, writers call on their readers to *recognize* a flaw in or to see the value of the subject matter. They denounce something or celebrate its worth—or do a little of both.
- Fixing (*It's Not Quite What We Thought*): As new discoveries get made, as new technology gets created or tossed aside, writers often find a way of tweaking a shared perspective. They are not out to change the fundamentals or to call for a different direction but merely to *tweak some prior approach or shared thinking*. For instance, in their work on climate change, some scientists have explained that deforestation rates have as much, if not more, impact as fossil fuels on the overall greenhouse effect. These scientists are not out to dismiss thousands of experiments and conclusions about climate change. Instead, they are explaining a slight misunderstanding in the field. They are fixing, not dismissing.
- Choosing a Side (*I'm Entering This Debate*): Popular, political, and educational cultures are full of debate. There are small, polite disagreements as well as long-term battles in which writers line up

and try to outmaneuver the opposition—or, in the best of all worlds, change their minds. Individual writers, at some point, decide where they stand on big unresolved conflicts. And quite often, they do so in a public manner. Usually, these arguments begin with a careful explanation of the debate. Then, the writer comes down on one side.

- Warning (*There's Danger Ahead!*): Many opinion pieces, academic articles, and argumentative blog posts are driven by the need to warn others of whatever is coming. Countless articles and books deal with impending crises. Economists, for instance, warn of future hits to financial institutions or international currency problems. Biologists warn of bacterial adaptation. Psychologists warn of seclusion. Biologists warn of super-bacteria.

- Proposing (*Here's a Better Way of Doing It*): Much public argumentation calls for action. Writers in all fields make a case that something needs to change, and so they describe the need and the specific way to address it. Sometimes, they even chart out particular steps for addressing a problem. They may establish the precise methods for making things better, or they might call for new thinking—a proposal to adopt a new mental framework.

- Transforming (*Let's Escape the Status Quo*): If people and institutions are to move forward, or in any direction, they must occasionally snap free from standard methods and conventional beliefs. Alone or together, humans do not change easily. They must be nudged, shouldered, and shoved out of their usual habits. Writers, then, often become the voices of dissent in their own disciplines or communities. They call on others to recognize a flaw in the usual way of doing things. And if that flaw is buried deep in shared beliefs or conventional wisdom, then the call for change can become insistent. (Chapter 8, "Escape the Status Quo" examines this process closely—as both a purpose in writing and a fundamental intellectual move.)

Of course, there are many more purposes. But these represent a large chunk of argumentative writing. And sometimes, purposes combine. Someone might, for instance, weigh in on a debate while also warning of danger ahead. The important point here is that a position can take many forms and that it always depends on a specific purpose.

Key Questions

Closely examine the argument under consideration and ask the following:

- Whether or not the writer/speaker is directly present in the text, what do they value? What do they want to happen?
- What do they assume or believe about the topic?
- What is the writer/speaker's purpose? Be as specific as possible in describing that purpose.

(4) Identifying Counterarguments, Concessions, Qualifiers

Most arguments address or manage opposing ideas. In other words, they acknowledge other possible claims about the issue. They may even grant value to those other claims or admit the limits of their own positions. Depending on the nature of the argument, the context, and even the topic itself, an argument may include lengthy passages of *counterarguments, concessions*, and *qualifiers*. Therefore, understanding these elements is crucial to good analysis.

Counterarguments: When arguers address an opposing position, they are *counterarguing*. In legal terms, they are offering a *rebuttal*. Done well, counterarguing can generate sophisticated ideas and rich passages. In written form, counterarguments often show up in two steps: (A) an explanation of an opposing position and (B) reasons why that opposing position is wrong (logically flawed, inaccurate, inhumane, unethical, or misguided in some way). For example, imagine an argument for foreign language study—why students should embrace foreign language requirements. Such an argument might include several passages that explain the benefits of foreign language courses. But it would also include counterarguments—passages that directly challenge the opposition. The following passage takes the two common steps for counterarguing. First, it explains a position against foreign language courses. Second, it explains why that position is wrong or what it "misses":

> Opponents of foreign language requirements argue that courses in French, German, Spanish and the like are impractical. They believe most students

will not find multilingual abilities useful. All the time committed to learning a foreign language, then, could have been spent learning more applicable skills, those that help young adults thrive in professional life. However, this notion misses a basic fact about professional life: it is increasingly international, which means it is increasingly multilingual. As new generations enter the workforce, they interact with people beyond their hometowns, beyond their communities, beyond their shores. A multilingual workforce is becoming a requirement for a range of companies.

As in this passage, counterarguments are often delivered as *turnabout paragraphs*, those that begin characterizing an opposing position and then turn against that position. Turnabouts begin with some typical phrases:

- Some argue . . .
- Opponents believe . . .
- Opponents of _____ say . . .
- Advocates of _____ argue . . .

The turnabout paragraph then pivots with a word or phrase signaling the writer's denial of the information or claim being described:

- However, . . .
- Contrarily, . . .
- But . . .
- This position misses . . .
- This claim ignores . . .
- This argument lacks . . .

Written arguments can include *multiple* turnabout paragraphs and may even devote several lengthy passages to the counter itself. In fact, counterarguments can account for the most sophisticated passages in an argument. And, as the next chapter explains, the best way to enrich an argument is by confronting sophisticated opponents.

Concessions: Concessions are related to counterarguments. While counterarguments deny or find fault with opposing positions, concessions grant them value. In other words, writers who concede simply acknowledge that *some opposing position has worth*. This doesn't throw off the original argument but shows the richness of opinions about the topic itself. (We do this often in everyday life. Whenever we acknowledge the value of someone else's position, we concede. In some respects, concessions make an argument sound more reasonable, more in touch with the world of ideas beyond the writer's own opinion.)

Concessions often come tucked between the two steps explained above (in the Counterarguments section). In other words, writers may grant some worth to an opposing position *before* denying part of its reasoning:

> *Opponents of foreign language requirements argue that courses in French, German, Spanish and the like are impractical. They believe most students will not find their multilingual abilities useful. All the time committed to learning a foreign language, then, could have been spent learning more applicable skills, those that help young adults thrive in professional life.* **While it's admirable to keep education practical, or at least connected to students' lives**, *this notion misses a basic fact about professional life: it is increasingly international, which means it is increasingly multilingual. As new generations enter the workforce, they interact with people beyond their hometowns, beyond their communities, beyond their shores. A multilingual workforce is quickly becoming a requirement for a range of companies.*

Sometimes, a concession can even steer the nature of the counterargument:

> *Opponents of foreign language requirements argue that courses in French, German, Spanish and the like are impractical. They believe most students will not find their multilingual abilities useful. All the time committed to learning a foreign language, then, could have been spent learning more applicable skills, those that help young adults thrive in professional life. While it's admirable to keep education practical, or at least connected to students' lives, practicality itself can lead educational policy down some unproductive paths. After all, calculus isn't all that practical for many students, nor is physics or philosophy. For that matter, history might even be characterized as impractical because most people are committed to their lives in the present and future. If practicality weighs too heavily on curriculum, a good number of important courses would get sidelined.*

Qualifiers: When someone qualifies a claim, they simply limit its scope. In other words, they are explaining *the limits of their own argument*. Qualifiers show up constantly in sophisticated arguments, and they demonstrate writers or speakers acknowledging the boundaries of their claims. As with counterarguments and concessions, we qualify constantly in everyday life:

- I'm not saying *all* cats are evil, just that Daniel's tabby cannot be trusted.
- Not all conservatives oppose environmental protection, but mainstream conservative policy has consistently turned against clean water protection.
- This is not a complaint against Michigan, but Ann Arbor sure has become unfriendly to outsiders.
- I'm not against all sports, but too many resources and energy have been consumed by high school football.

In formal arguments, qualifiers can come in many forms—as brief statements or lengthy passages that detail exceptions:

- Brief: While not all students should be required to take multiple years of foreign language, those who plan on attending college or moving into the professional workforce should get at least two years of focused study.
- Detailed: Not all students should be required to take multiple years of foreign language. After all, some have declared their intentions for vocational training and seek specialized skills in a trade. While they may go onward in post-secondary education, they may not benefit, at least in the short term, from language study. Their chosen path does not warrant significant time involved in language acquisition.

Analyzing an argument means identifying all these elements and explaining their function. When we can fully explain the role of counterarguments, concessions, and qualifiers, we get a sense of the main argumentative ingredients.

Key Questions

After closely reading the target argument, consider the following:

- Where does the writer/speaker challenge opposing ideas (counterargue)?
- Where does the writer/speaker grant value to an opposing idea (concede)?

- Where does the writer/speaker express the limits or scope of their position (qualify)?

Activity Prompts: (1) In a small group, share a time when you granted value to someone else's point, even if you disagreed with their overall position. In other words, explain a situation when you admitted that someone else had a good idea even if you argued against them. (2) As a class, divide into several small groups. Debate a public issue. Despite anyone's particular position, take a group stance on the issue and develop a claim. Then develop at least two reasons for your claim. After hearing the other groups' claims, develop counterarguments, concessions, and/or qualifiers and share them with the class.

(5) Analyzing the Audience

When we say *audience*, we don't mean the specific people reading an argument at a given time. We mean the people who would most likely sit through, listen to, or read the argument—the people who have certain values, attitudes, knowledge, and expectations that would make them apt to tune in. Of course, we usually don't have direct access to the audience of an argument. We can't look at them as though they were all seated in a theater. We can't ask them what they believe, what they value, what they know. But we can discover a good deal about an audience by considering the publication and language of the argument.

Publication simply means the magazine, publisher, or website that brought the text into public view. Each publication has its style and tendencies. *Family Circle*, a moderately conservative magazine for women with families, is not likely to publish an argument on the glories of body piercing. On the other hand, the *Body Piercing* Journal will likely not publish an article about nicely shaded back porches where families can gather in the evenings. In short, we can conclude a great deal about the audience by looking at the publisher of an argument. We can sense the kinds of attitudes and values within that audience.

If we are analyzing an online article, we can also find out a good deal by quickly inspecting the publisher's own statements. Most magazine and news websites include an *About* tab that expresses editorial information. For example, *Utne Reader*, a popular magazine, describes itself in the following way:

> **Utne Reader** and **Utne.com** *are digests of independent ideas and alternative culture. Not right, not left, but forward thinking. We're most interested in creating a conversation about everything from the environment to the economy, politics to pop culture.*

Imagine we're examining an argument about student debt, one published in Utne Reader. As a "forward-thinking" magazine, it is probably sympathetic to student debt. An article in such a magazine wouldn't have to convince readers that huge amounts of student debt are bad. (And the latter section of this chapter explains, a like-minded or sympathetic audience impacts the nature of an argument: what it must do, what it must include, and what it might safely exclude.)

Publication can also suggest something about the expertise level of the audience. An audience for a scholarly journal has a high degree of expertise and disciplinary knowledge. For example, an article in the *Journal of Chemical Physics* targets physicists—and physicists only. Writers in such a journal assume their readers will zoom along at high speeds while recalling all the experiments and theories that are referenced. They don't worry about explaining big terms. Contrarily, when news channels publish an article about some new scientific discovery, they avoid jargon and/or try to fill in important background information for readers.

Activity Prompt: In a small group, discuss the following argumentative passage about student loans. Even if you don't know where the argument was published, you can probably determine something about the audience. Describe the primary audience—its values, hopes, or needs:

> *Elected officials in government have essentially abandoned college students. They have abdicated their duty to represent all the electorate—not simply the seniors who tend to vote in much greater numbers than traditional college students. While they listen to banks and financial institution lobbyists, members of Congress and the state legislature have lost touch with the citizens working to enter the shrinking middle class.*

(6) Advanced Move: Calling Out Unstated Reasons

As a previous section explains, analyzing arguments involves identifying the reasons for a writer's position or claim. This process can be especially tricky because not all reasons are stated. Many reasons, in fact, go *unstated* because the speaker/writer assumes that readers will automatically accept them. Even though they are not written or stated directly, they still matter. For example, let's return to the college loan topic from a previous section. The following passage states reasons for making student loans interest-free.

> *Most students today simply cannot pay for college, nor can their parents. In fact, paying for a full four-year degree is now far beyond the ability of nearly all American families. Only the very wealthy can pay for an entire college education, which means nearly all college students graduate with some form of debt, which stretches into decades or over lifetimes. Because a generation of debtors is bad for the overall economy, student loans should, at the least, be interest-free.*

Charted out, the reasoning of this passage looks like this:

Claim: Student loans should be interest-free.

Reasons:

   Most college students cannot pay for college and, therefore, must get loans.

   Most college students will graduate with major loan debt.

   A majority of college students shouldn't graduate with growing debt.

   A generation of debtors is bad for the economy.

There's also an unstated reason at work, something so widely accepted that the writer feels no need to state it: *Anything bad for the economy should be changed*. In other words, the writer assumes that readers will automatically accept that point and so leaves it unsaid. This doesn't mean the writer is wrong or that the argument falls short. It simply means that the argument relies on an unstated reason. Even though a writer may not express all reasons, they are often part of the argument—part of the quiet operations of an argument. That's how reasoning works: while some points are expressed, other points sometimes hover quietly in the background. And this is not necessarily bad or wrong. But if we're dismantling an argument (or writing one), we should try to understand all elements—the unstated and the stated.

As this example shows, reasoning depends to some degree on context, on what has been said, on what the audience believes, and on what arguer and audience assume. In other words, those attitudes and concerns that surround any given argument shape the reasoning. The writer/speaker and audience are always interacting in subtle ways. The nature of that interaction determines what gets said or left unsaid.

Key Question

After carefully reading the argument under consideration, ask the following: What reasons are suggested but not necessarily stated?

Sample Analysis

The following essay examines an article published in the New York Times, 2022, after President Biden announced a targeted college loan forgiveness program. At the time, Biden's proposal was widely debated and covered in mainstream news outlets. The essay begins by describing that broader situation (context). It goes on to analyze the reasoning and counterarguments operating in the article. It also briefly explains the role of the writer and audience.

> *In "Why I Changed My Mind on Debt Forgiveness," Susan Dynarski makes a case for President Biden's plan to forgive millions of dollars in college loans. The issue affects not only current college students but future students, their families, and anyone who might seek out financial support for higher education. When Biden proposed his plan, it was met with both relief and ridicule. Thousands of former college students celebrated the idea while political opponents argued it would move financial responsibility from college graduates to American taxpayers. In other words, college debt was a heated issue. Dynarski's article addresses this friction directly.*
>
>   *Dynarski's title says much about her purpose. She's correcting her own thinking on a widely debated issue, but in a subtle way, she's also arguing against anyone who might still hold her former position. In other words, her entire article is an indirect counterargument. Because she announces herself as*

an economist, she suggests that her previous position was probably reasonable and informed, which means her new position is even more reasonable and more informed. Given her change of heart on the issue, she discusses the most important information that shifted her thinking.

Her main claim is stated directly. In short, she supports targeted debt cancellation. In her introductory passages, she lists her reasons thoroughly. She argues for targeted debt cancellation because (A) the funding system is broken and has been for decades, (B) college tuition continues to increase, which means student borrow continues to increase, and (C) students face increasing financial harm as they work to cover mounting costs.

As her argument continues, she takes on each reason, starting with the "broken" college funding system. To support her point, she must characterize an entire funding process as flawed. Therefore, several passages include the mathematics of rising tuition, decreased state funding, and average pay for part-time college workers. All this evidence works to show that college students can no longer pay for school by working as they did generations ago. This historical point suggests something else, something unstated but central to the debate about funding and forgiveness. While Dynarki doesn't say it directly, she implies that paying for college has surpassed even the most hardworking students. The costs have gone far beyond any individual's ability to manage them. Therefore, one cannot blame students for debt, especially if that debt came with no benefits.

Dynarski then works to describe student borrowers, especially the type most injured by debt. They are not, most often, graduates of elite institutions but those who took some college credits at local community colleges or for-profit online schools. In other words, the most serious debtors are those without advanced degrees—and without the earning power to pay off loans. She argues that such students did not benefit from their college credits and were even exploited by institutions' efforts to drive up their own enrollments. This section of her argument, then, is counterargument. She is directly challenging politicians and pundits who raged against debt forgiveness because it helps graduates of elite colleges—those with great salaries and assets. Her evidence works against that notion.

The final third of Dynarski's article returns to the funding system itself. She gives a brief historical account of student debt. This account draws attention to increasing interest rates, few options for students, and decreasing government support. In other words, she argues that college costs have skyrocketed along with the price of getting a loan. This section of the argument, then, works to draw attention away from individual borrowers and to shed light on a system designed to undermine students, especially those who need funding the most.

> Finally, Dynarski's argument was published by the New York Times and still remains on the NYT website. The New York Times readership is well-read, highly literate, and interested in public policy statements, so it makes sense that Dynarski's article delves into the particulars of funding policy. It's not simply an argument for helping poorer students but one that critiques years of "broken" policy.

(7) Advanced Move: Calling Out the Quiet Argument

Arguments don't always look like arguments. In fact, they can stow away in other things—questions, jokes, stories, songs, films, and pieces of fine art. This doesn't mean that *everything* you encounter is an argument. It means some things besides written and spoken arguments can *assert something about the world*. For example, a movie such as *Juno* (2007) asserts something about the emotional and social struggles of teen pregnancy. The *Harry Potter* series asserts something about the power of fellowship to challenge evil.

If we can develop our radar, we can detect and analyze the quiet arguments around us. The process is a bit different from the process of analyzing a written argument. We're not looking for stated and unstated reasons but elements that build up to a claim—details that accumulate and express something. For example, in the *Harry Potter* series, there's no single scene that states unequivocally how fellowship can undermine evil. Instead, many scenes and situations suggest that claim. The same can be said about other films, literary works, pieces of art, and even architecture. Restaurants, libraries, museums, and so on are designed to suggest ideas about the business inside. Of course, buildings themselves do not "speak," but all the structural details can add up to a message. The following passage explains how a coffee shop argues a point:

> *The Coffee House makes clear, both inside and out, that simple is good. Positioned at the corner of Main and Clark Street, the building's exterior is plain brown siding, literally the color of coffee, with a windowless wooden door. The interior offers a bar with ten cushioned stools, five tables, and three conventional sofas. Walls feature four large landscape paintings, nothing abstract or visually confusing, only mountains, a sunset, a forest, and a lake.*

*It's art that might be considered unfancy, pleasant, and easy-on-the-eyes. The place is lit by standing lamps with thick iron posts, nothing ornate or delicate. Finally, the menu itself says, over and over, that drinking coffee should not require much thinking. Sizes are **small**, **medium**, and **large**—no French terms, no tricky suggestions. Drinks are listed in order: coffee (light, medium, dark, and decaf), latte, cappuccino, and espresso.*

The Coffee House does not claim, in written language, that coffee should be simple, but the passage draws out the details, the exterior and interior elements that accumulate or add up to that claim. Writers in all fields make this three-part move: (1) they closely inspect the details of a building, film, literary work, even something as big and ill-defined as a city; (2) they find a pattern in those details that suggests an argument; and (3) they express that argument in writing.

Activity Prompt: School architecture makes claims. The structures and geography indirectly assert ideas about learning, education, enlightenment, authority, and so on. The paved roads winding their way around a building might suggest, "Be careful here." The columns at an entryway might say something about the grand tradition of the school and its history. In a small group, consider a piece of architecture from your school building. Closely inspect the details and find a pattern that suggests an argument. Do the details add up to some point about education, freedom, learning, or hardship? Also consider the context. What is the relationship between the subject and the surroundings? Do they complement one another or oppose one another? Try to express that argument in writing.

Writing Prompts

1. Examine a specific written argument—an article, blog post, or even the transcript of a speech. Use the following steps to help you analyze the argument. You need not take on every step or question here. A detailed explanation of one of these points may launch your examination and provide sufficient momentum.

    - Check the cultural temperature: what issues are heated or debated? Why is this topic or particular argument important? How do you know?

- Examine the publication. Does it suggest or state anything about its values?
- Identify the topic, main claim, and supporting reasons.
- What unstated reasons can you detect? Are they widely accepted? (Would most readers of this argument accept them?)
- Take some aspect of the argument (either a major claim or some supporting reason) and show its relationship to some other part of the argument.
- Who is writing? How does the writer construct his or her authority to argue on this topic?
- What is the writer's purpose? What language makes it clear?
- Who is being targeted? What are their expectations and assumptions?
- How does the publication figure in? What does it tell you about the audience?
- Is the audience hostile or friendly? Already knowledgeable about the issue or in need of being taught? Does the nature of the topic require treading lightly around the audience's attitudes? Or can the writer go forward and not worry about offending readers or encountering resistance?

2. Choose a nontextual (unwritten) work, such as a work of art or architecture. Examine the quiet argument that the work is making. In an essay, analyze the message of the work. How does the message relate to the work's purpose? Consider how people use the work. How, if at all, has the work's purpose changed over time? Here, also think about the context surrounding the work. Where is the work, and how does its physical setting affect its purpose? Its message? How might the surrounding cultural atmosphere or political climate affect the argument that the work is making?

4 Justifying a Position

As the previous chapter explains, argumentative writing is a mainstay in language arts classes and in first-year college. It is fundamental across grade levels and institutions. With so much emphasis and training, students still acquire some writerly habits that can muddle their efforts. For instance, students often begin an argumentative writing project by lunging for a position within an established two-sided debate. And when it comes to developing an essay, they may first and foremost seek numerical evidence to support their initial positions. Neither impulse is inherently bad, but argumentative includes a great deal more.

When writers take a position, they privilege one way of thinking above others. They say, in effect, "This is the best path." Despite all the other possibilities, they deem one more worthy. But how is it more worthy? Is it more sophisticated, clearheaded, logical, compassionate, practical, relevant, productive, or inclusive? Is the position more responsive to the facts? Is it more in line with surrounding trends? Will acting on it hurt the fewest people? Save the most? Such questions help writers embrace the complexity of an argument and, ultimately, make their work more sophisticated.

This chapter focuses exclusively on the moves that build to thoughtful positions, but it's not all that different from other chapters. While there are many and varied strategies for developing and delivering arguments, this chapter stays focused on some key moves: (1) adopting a position and purpose, (2) breaking down the reasons, (3) providing evidence, (4) managing the opposition, (5) seeking reasons for reasons. (Note: argumentative writing may also involve moves from other chapters—seeking complexity, seeking tension, applying concepts, and so on. Please see Chapter 10: Mapping the Moves for additional guidance on combining moves from various chapters.)

(1) Adopting a Position and Purpose

The *position* is the stance of the writer—the single idea that must be established and justified with sound reasons. And that position depends on a *purpose*—the overall motivation of the argument. Are we out to condemn something? Fix something? Propose a new way of thinking? While arguing a point may seem like a purpose, writing gets more focused and more powerful when a purpose is narrow. Consider the list of purposes from Chapter 3:

- Supporting or Condemning (*This Is ... or Isn't ... a Good Idea*): These arguments call on readers to recognize a flaw in or to see the value of the subject matter. They denounce something or celebrate its worth—or, as is the case most often, do a little of both.
- Fixing (*It's Not Quite What We Thought*): In these arguments, writers are not out to change the fundamentals or to call for a different direction but to amend some prior approach or shared thinking.
- Choosing a Side (*I'm Weighing In on This Debate*): These arguments begin with a careful explanation of the debate. Then, the writer comes down on one side and breaks down her reasons.
- Warning (*There's Danger Ahead!*): In these arguments, writers set out to warn others of whatever is coming. Such arguments are often based on past and present trends.
- Proposing (*Here's a Better Way of Doing It*): In these arguments, writers make a case that something needs to change, so they describe the need and the specific way to address it. Sometimes, they even chart out particular steps for addressing a problem.
- Transforming (*Let's Escape the Status Quo*): In these arguments, writers call on their readers to recognize a flaw in the usual way of doing

things. And if that flaw is buried deep in the workings of a field, then the call for change can become insistent.

Purposes often depend on the context and audience—who's potentially listening, who's invested in the topic, who's potentially at odds with the writer's position, and what other positions have been expressed. In short, the situation matters. Writers have to ask themselves what kind of argument would work best, which would be best received, and which would have the most impact. For instance, choosing a side in a debate may be worthless if the debate itself is flawed. Instead, the writer might be better off escaping it altogether and promoting an entirely different position. Similarly, a writer might decide that proposing a solution can wait because the problem itself needs to be understood first—or the problem has been wrongly defined by others.

Key Question

Consider your current writing project. Even if your teacher has assigned a topic, try to explain your specific purpose: What is your argument trying to accomplish? The answer will help you make a range of other decisions, such as what you will research, what kind of information is most important, what other positions you should consider, and what concepts are most relevant.

(2) Breaking Down the Reasons

Positions need *reasons*—statements that justify a given position. Reasons are the *whys* of an argumentative position. Writers should always try to break down and articulate their reasons, which can be a challenge, especially when we are deeply committed to a position. It can be like untangling a ball of rope or trying to find the beginning of a tape spool. We must scratch away until we find some beginning point, some basic understanding of our own thinking. So how do we begin? How do we discover the *why* behind our positions? We can take a cue from the Declaration of Independence, which is famous not simply for starting a revolution but also for breaking down the reasons for that revolution. It begins with something that the founding fathers believed to be "self-evident" or beyond question:

> *We hold these truths to be self-evident, that all men are created equal, that they are endowed by their Creator with certain unalienable Rights, that among these are Life, Liberty and the pursuit of Happiness. —That to secure these rights, Governments are instituted among Men, deriving their just powers from the consent of the governed, —That whenever any Form of Government becomes destructive of these ends, it is the Right of the People to alter or to abolish it, and to institute new Government, laying its foundation on such principles and organizing its powers in such form, as to them shall seem most likely to effect their Safety and Happiness.*

So the American Revolution gets launched with a general statement about equality and the role of governments to protect it. That, according to the Declaration, is the first reason for American independence. To argue that the colonists should be free from tyranny, Thomas Jefferson (the primary author of the Declaration) needed the general point that "all men," not just the colonial men, should be free from tyranny. Once that point is established, Jefferson goes on to list specific situations that oppose it. The King of England, Jefferson explains, kept colonists from making decisions about their own communities, kept British soldiers in the colonial towns, and forced colonists to pay for their own harassment. After listing the specifics, Jefferson concludes:

> *We, therefore, the Representatives of the united States of America, in General Congress, Assembled, appealing to the Supreme Judge of the world for the rectitude of our intentions, do, in the Name, and by Authority of the good People of these Colonies, solemnly publish and declare, That these united Colonies are, and of Right ought to be Free and Independent States, that they are Absolved from all Allegiance to the British Crown, and that all political connection between them and the State of Great Britain, is and ought to be totally dissolved; ...*

With the Declaration as an example, we can see that argumentative reasoning is often driven by some *principle* of right and wrong, some general belief about what should or shouldn't happen, or some general understanding of behavior. This is not to say that reasoning *must* begin at such a broad level. In fact, if every position on every topic were connected to statements as broad as "all men are created equal," it would get difficult to express our reasons. But reasoning in writing (and in our daily lives) often relies on some principle. To justify our positions, we often need an idea that *extends beyond* the specific situation.

Here's another way to think about it: in some respects, reasoning is an audience issue. Since the Declaration of Independence was written for a big audience (people throughout the colonies, aristocrats in England, and government officials throughout Europe), it had to do more than express the American colonists' concerns. It had to *connect those concerns to a broader principle*, one that people in England, France, and Spain could consider and understand. Reasoning, in this sense, is the acknowledgment that other people's brains are involved.

Activity Prompts: (1) The founding fathers understood that "all men" of European descent were equal. It took nearly two centuries before women and non-European men were acknowledged equally under American law. As a class, try to break down the reasons behind the idea that all people (regardless of wealth, race, sex, or sexual orientation) should be treated equally under the law. Consider instances in which the law does not treat individuals equally, such as age (children who may not vote, teenagers who commit violent crimes), status (citizens vs. noncitizens), or sexual orientation (same-sex couples who may not marry). (2) Discuss the *context* of the Declaration of Independence. Remember that the Declaration was written at the end of the eighteenth century. The audience included American colonists, English aristocrats, and heads of state throughout Europe. Jefferson and his colleagues were seeking freedom from King George's control. Beyond the obvious tensions, what can you sense? What ideas may have been heated, new, or potentially unacceptable? How do you know?

For another example, let's return to the student loan topic raised in the previous chapter. If we were to argue that college loans should be interest-free, we would need reasons. The following list would generate various passages for an argument:

Claim: College loans should be interest-free.

Reasons:

- Most college students cannot pay for college and must get loans.
- Most college students will graduate with major loan debt.
- A majority of college students shouldn't graduate with major debt.
- A generation of debtors is bad for the economy.

Each bulleted statement helps to justify the claim. Taken together, the statements build a *line of reasoning* that creates an argument. A writer could explain and support the reasons separately, devoting a paragraph or more to each. In this way, charting out one's reasons can be a powerful and practical way to organize an essay.

For a final example, let's return to the foreign language topic from the previous chapter. While many different positions could be taken within that topic, our argument favors two years of language study. Someone might argue that foreign language study gives students a better sense of grammar and, therefore, a deeper understanding of their own language. That reasoning could generate an entire argument. But let's pursue another set of reasons, those that connect foreign language to professional life:

> Claim: High school students should take at least two full years of a foreign language.
>
> Reasons:
> - Workplaces are increasingly diverse and globalized.
> - Foreign language proficiency gives native English speaking students ability to communicate in an increasingly diverse and globalized workplace.
> - Foreign language study gives native English speakers a better sense of others' attitudes and beliefs.
> - Understanding others' attitudes and beliefs helps coworkers to succeed at work.

What's key is that our reasons are related. These are not *all* the possible benefits of foreign language study. Instead, they are interconnected reasons that build toward the claim. In fact, the first two and last two form mini *lines of reasoning*. They justify one another. It's easy to imagine someone asking why each reason matters—and finding the answer in the next:

- Workplaces are increasingly diverse and globalized.
  - Why does that matter?

- Foreign language proficiency gives native English speaking students ability to communicate in an increasingly diverse and globalized workplace.
  - Why does that matter?

- Communicating well with others helps coworkers succeed.

- Foreign language study gives native English speakers a better sense of others' attitudes and beliefs.
    - Why does that matter?
- Understanding others' attitudes and beliefs helps coworkers succeed.

Key Question

To develop reasons for your argument, try to list separate ideas that come from asking this single question: what must people believe before they accept my claim?

(3) Providing Evidence

Reasons alone are often insufficient for a sound argument. Reasons usually need some help in the form of *evidence*: facts, data, testimony, and anecdotes. Evidence is information from the world beyond the argument. It is out there in studies, experiments, and reports. It is part of history, part of the record beyond anyone's position:

- Fact: information that has been proven or something known to be true.
- Statistic: information delivered in numerical form.
- Testimony: information delivered from the person or people who directly experienced or observed something.
- Anecdote: a brief story about a real event or person.

Of course, evidence can be disputed. Data can be questioned and thrown out. Testimony can be dismissed. In fact, disputing evidence is its own kind of argument—the kind in which people inspect the soundness of information or the methods that generate it. However, we don't have to abandon evidence simply because it can be questioned. Even though facts and data are disputable, they are often necessary for supporting our reasons and, therefore, justifying our positions.

Evidence takes on its argumentative force when it supports a specific reason. For example, consider our first bit of reasoning in the foreign language argument: *The workplace is increasingly diverse.* This idea wants proof—evidence that shows increasing diversity within the workplace. If we know we must reinforce this point, we can easily find helpful information. In fact, the other reasons in our foreign language argument could also benefit from different forms of evidence:

- Reason: Workplaces are increasingly diverse and globalized.
    - Evidence: Facts and statistics that show increasing ethnic, national, and linguistic diversity.
- Reason: Foreign language proficiency gives native English speaking students ability to communicate in an increasingly diverse and globalized workplace.
    - Evidence: Facts, testimony, and/or anecdotes that connect foreign language courses with language proficiency.
- Reason: Foreign language study gives native English speakers a better sense of others' attitudes and beliefs.
    - Evidence: Facts, testimony, and/or anecdotes that connect foreign language courses with a better sense of others' attitudes and beliefs.
- Reason: Understanding others' attitudes and beliefs helps coworkers to succeed at work.
    - Evidence: Facts, testimony, and/or anecdotes that connect understanding coworkers with professional success.

Arguments often develop according to this pattern. The writer expresses a reason and then devotes a full paragraph (or several paragraphs) to supporting that reason. Then the writer moves to the next reason, and so on. In book-length arguments, writers often devote *entire chapters* to each reason. They provide various forms of evidence to make that reason as acceptable as possible.

Activity Prompt: Daniel Patrick Moynihan, a four-term United States senator, famously said, "You are entitled to your own opinions but not your own facts." He was responding to the practice of choosing some facts and ignoring others, or to simply making up information that supports one's own worldview. Have you witnessed that reflex? Have you seen or heard people selecting and fashioning facts so that they can maintain their position? In a small group, discuss your experiences.

(4) Managing the Opposition

Whenever writers are justifying a position, they must consider all the other positions swirling around. We can't just ignore them! We must explain why they're wrong and why our position is better. It's not enough to say, "You're wrong." We must break down other positions and explain why they're less practical, less accurate, less humane, and so on. And that's where all the steps from Chapter 3 come in. The more thoroughly we break down and explain the logic of the opposition, the more intact and sound our own position becomes. (Note: Chapter 3 explains the following elements in more detail.)

Counterarguments: Simply put, a counterargument is the act of refuting an opposing position. Whatever the topic, writers arguing a position must take on the opposition—anyone who would challenge the position in the first place. Counterarguments are often delivered in *turnabout paragraphs*. The writer begins by characterizing an opposing position, then pivots with a term such as *however, contrarily*, or *but*. The paragraph ends by calling out the shortcomings or flaw in that opposing position.

Concessions: When writers acknowledge the value of an opposing position, they are *conceding*. This doesn't make their arguments less valid. In fact, concessions can make an argument more reasonable and more sophisticated.

Qualifiers: When writers acknowledge the limits of their own claims, they are qualifying. In other words, they are admitting that their claim does not apply to all situations or to everyone. Qualifiers make an argument more sound, less open to doubt, and less vulnerable to opposition. In this sense, qualifiers fill potential leaks in our argumentative boats.

(5) Advanced Move: Seeking Reasons for Reasons

Sometimes, a position can be justified for a single but powerful reason. For example, if someone tells you to run from the building because it's on fire, you don't need a second or third reason. One is enough! But when it comes to many other topics, writers need to crack open the reasons and seek out more subtle thinking inside them. In fact, the best thinking often comes along when we get beyond the obvious reasons—the ones that we automatically conjure, the ones we've heard over and over in other arguments. For example, we could take one of the reasons from our foreign language argument and break it down further. The following passage takes on our third reason and does just that:

> *Foreign language study gives native English speakers a better sense of others' attitudes and beliefs. When coworkers understand one another's attitudes, workplace goals are much easier to accomplish. It's difficult, in fact, to work well with others without some deep understanding of their basic beliefs and attitudes. But there's another layer, something beyond collaboration. It's much easier to sell an idea, service, or product with a basic understanding of other people—what they believe in principle and practice. Of course, beliefs often transcend language and culture. People of all stripes (and tongues) grapple with right and wrong, often in strikingly similar ways. But some beliefs are concealed away from others. They live in the language, deep in words, phrases, and clauses.*

This is a difficult move because our initial reasons are often common reasons—those that seem obvious, big, and undeniable. We have to get beyond the automatic power of those reasons and imagine the many possible ideas within them. We might then see how something works, how something might be specifically harmful or helpful. We might even see some subtle layer of thinking that others have missed altogether.

Key Question

Consider one of the reasons for your claim—anything you've stated that explains why your position is best. And then ask this basic question: why is that reason valuable, sound, or especially important? If you can answer this question in a paragraph, you will be developing a reason for a reason.

Writing Prompts

When good questions can be raised, positions must be justified. When there's more than one obvious answer, we have to work through the ideas and chart them out. As you consider your own project, take one of the following paths:

1. Many argumentative positions depend on some principle of fairness. Consider a situation in which someone or some group of people was not treated fairly. Write an essay that condemns the unfair policy or action. As you develop reasoning for your position, seek out a source that offers an explanation of fairness. Apply specific language from that source to the specific situation.
2. Try a "fixing" argument. Go back to a previous era in your life—to early adolescence or elementary school—and describe a way of thinking that you were taught or that you accepted simply by virtue of living in a time and place. Explain how that thinking was flawed or flat-out wrong. Without dismissing the entire way of thinking, fix that flaw.
3. Try a "proposing" argument. Take on a specific practice in education (such as using standard print textbooks or sitting in rows). Explain what's wrong with that practice—the thinking behind it, the practical shortcomings of it. And then propose a better way. Make a case for that better way. Explain why it's more agile, helpful, practical, efficient, or even humane.
4. Often, written arguments are not full-scale wars or even battles. They are drawn-out examinations of an issue that involve different, and sometimes opposing, perspectives. Consider a practice that is widely accepted in education (such as online writing courses or separating subjects into different classrooms) and develop a position about the value of that practice. Why is it worth continuing, or why might teachers want to reconsider it? Rather than dismiss potential opposition, include other perspectives in your reasoning.

5 Applying Sources

Integrating sources is key to formal writing. Sources help students to engage a world of opinion and information. The process comes with a long list of pitfalls, strange encumbrances, and rules that leave students reeling. In fact, when students move into research, source integration, citation, and documentation, they sometimes lose the creative, the inventive, and the more vital elements of writing. But sources needn't be fraught with difficulty. They can be powerful building blocks and much more.

It's important, then, to think of sources as *sources of thought*—voices that change, flip, thicken, bolster, and counter a writer's own ideas. Describing sources as intellectual catalysts opens up possibilities for incorporating research into student writing. In fact, sources can help students make any writerly move. In other words, sources don't belong to any particular type of project or to any particular writerly purpose. A source might help a writer break up a duality, explain the tension surrounding a topic, analyze someone else's argument, justify a position, change the terms of a debate, or even escape the status quo. Or a source might simply provide some intellectual momentum. This chapter focuses on the following common moves for using sources: (1) applying a supportive source, (2) drawing from a vital source, (3) synthesizing sources, (4) drawing from the past, (5) trusting but verifying, and (6) citing sources.

(1) Applying a Supportive Source

As other chapters have explained, good writers *seek complexity*. They look for interesting tension, loose ends, unanswered questions, and exceptions to the rules. Sources can help with those ends. By adding dimension to our own ideas, sources clarify what we don't yet know, and they may even contradict what we think we know. In other words, sources make good thinking happen. Whether it's an article, report, book, literary work, blog, wiki, or an interview, a powerful source can get us out of our own head and connect us with other currents of thought.

Applying a supportive source may be the most basic and common move. Simply put, a supportive source reinforces a writer's ideas. When writers feel the need to link their own thinking with the ideas of others, they use a source to say, in effect, "It's not just me. Other people share my perspective." The source backs up the writer's position and connects it to a world of other people. For example, consider an essay that examines the role of mythology in modern movies. The following passage makes a claim and then offers a quotation from a supportive source:

> Movies have become our main form of shared entertainment. Millions of people flock to theaters every week to see the latest stories and the newest heroes. But all these films add up to something beyond entertainment. They carry an important role far more critical than casual weekend enjoyment. They do something for our shared beliefs, hopes, and basic questions. In **Movies Are**

> *Life,* Joan Miller says, "mainstream movies provide a shared understanding of our society, even our world."

Sources often get used in this fashion. When writers need more language and more scholarly force to establish a less obvious idea, they rely on sources. In other words, we don't simply drop in sources for the obvious points. We rely on others *when the thinking gets harder*, when the subject matter gets more vague or foggy, and when we're in need of more precise terms.

Activity Prompt: Consider a subject you're interested in. Choose a topic (such as the role of children in TV advertising, intimacy in social networking, or prescription drug addiction) and do some research on it. Locate at least two sources and explain in a sentence what each contributes to your thinking about the topic. How might each be used as a supportive source in an essay?

(2) Drawing from a Vital Source

Good writers rely on powerful sources, not only to support their initial thoughts but to build new and compelling insights. In other words, whenever we find an especially powerful voice (whether it's a report, essay, blog, book, or literary work), we can use it to launch and propel our own thinking. In fact, using a source as an intellectual springboard is a typical strategy. Millions of articles and books begin with a direct reference to a source that the writer found especially inspiring. From there, the writer takes up the source's idea and runs with it. The following passage illustrates one tried-and-true strategy. It introduces the topic, then the source. The passage ends with some key thinking from the source—a phrase that can be helpful as the writer continues onward.

> *Do the stories of ancient gods and heroes still matter? Can they offer anything beyond entertainment? According to famed mythographer Joseph Campbell, ancient myths reveal the most fundamental tensions of everyday life. Stories from thousands of years ago and from different cultures have much in common with one another and with modern existence. In* **The Hero's Adventure***, Campbell describes a "typical hero sequence of actions" that emerge from different civilizations and moments in history.*

In this way, an essay can begin by introducing a vital source such as Joseph Campbell. But we don't have to leave Campbell behind. If that source has many important and relevant insights, we can *come back around* to it. We can continue to draw ideas and apply them. In this case, we are following steps from Chapter 3, Applying a Concept. The concept comes from our vital source and allows us to explore:

> *Modern American life seems far removed from ancient myths—those old tales of heroes battling monsters, clear lines between good and evil, the consequences apparent for everyone. Today, our daily battles seem far more complex. Our enemies aren't single monsters but entire systems or institutions—insurance, banking, higher education—that seek to exploit us our siphon away our resources. The systems that work against us cannot be defeated with one victorious battle. In fact, they cannot be defeated at all. They're too big, too important to the social order. But even in this world of institutional monsters, there may still be room for heroes, for all of us to imagine "a typical hero sequence of actions."*

As the passage shows, we can borrow a concept from the vital source (Campbell) and explore the topic further. We can take language from the source and use it to explore our topic. In this case, we'll take "sequence of actions" and apply the phrase to modern life:

> *When we see our daily actions in the light of myth, we can understand their significance, our own significance. Campbell explains that heroes must leave home; they must set out on a journey. Their heroism cannot emerge until they've left the comforts of familiarity. Their departure, however, need not be seen literally. Leaving home can simply mean leaving behind everything that anchors us. If we are to become the hero of our own lives, our own survival, it means we must abandon what makes us most comfortable, most at ease— not forever but long enough to venture away and confront something bigger.*

The vital source propels us forward. Each time we *come back around* to Campbell's ideas, our own thinking gets deeper. This is a powerful strategy for developing intellectual richness: the writer devotes an opening paragraph, or several opening paragraphs, to a vital source and then continues to return to it. Applying the source involves more than simply referencing it and then moving on. It involves several steps: (1) summarizing the source, (2) explaining how the source sheds particular light on the issue at hand, and (3) weaving the insights from that source into one's own thinking. It's that third step, the weaving, that successful writers and readers are most interested in. The big insights often come when writers keep going back to a source—when they let it feed into each new idea they develop.

A Brief Look at Summary, Paraphrase, and Quotation

Summarizing, paraphrasing, and quoting are common practices in academic writing. They are used to portray what others have thought or said. There are many tricks, variables, and rules for each, but here are some key points about these critical practices:

> *The Key to Summary: It's all about precision. When we summarize, we describe someone else's ideas while also condensing them into our own words. But when we shorten something, we change it. So the trick of good summary is to hand over the most accurate version possible—to describe the heart of the work (the movie, book, article, or whatever it may be) that distinguishes it from all other similar works. It's a balancing act between brevity and accuracy. On one hand, we don't want to boil things down so that the original idea is barely distinguishable from a million other things. On the other, we don't want to drag things out too long and end up retelling a whole story or argument. Check out the differences among three summaries below:*
>
> *Too General: Harry Potter is the story of a kid with no parents.*
> *Too Brief: Harry Potter is the story of an orphaned boy with magical powers.*
> *Short but Accurate: Harry Potter is the story of a young wizard who must discover his own power and use it to destroy the ultimate evil force in the world.*
>
> *Most often, academic writers summarize an article or book in a few sentences. They don't drag things out too long because they've got other business to attend to. They're trying, after all, to **do** something with the summary. They're using it to build a point, to develop an insight of their own.*
>
> *The Key to Paraphrase: Like summary, paraphrase involves rewording ideas from a source, but in paraphrase, the goal is **not** to condense or abbreviate. In other words, paraphrasing means re-explaining exactly what a source has already said without using the direct phrases from the source. It can be tricky work. If writers aren't careful, they may end up borrowing sentences and phrases without quoting them. In academic and professional situations, that's considered plagiarism. On the other hand, good paraphrase can be a powerful*

*move—a way to thoroughly understand and give our own voice to the ideas that we learned from a source. In fact, some of the best writing happens when someone carefully reads a source, understands the source at a deep level, and then articulates that understanding in a genuinely different way—with different comparisons, images, and descriptions. The goal is to lend our own voice to the ideas in that source. (Paraphrase must **still** be cited. See the final section of this chapter.)*

*The Key to Quotation. Writers quote for many reasons—to show what an opponent thinks, to show what supporters say, to show the exact words of an important theorist, and so on. Regardless of the purpose, quoting should **highlight the most critical or the most important language from a source**. We do this constantly in our daily lives. When we're describing a song to someone, we don't sing a few lines from the fourth verse. We sing the chorus—the key words and melody that make the song what it is. In academic writing, quotation works in the same way. Writers home in on the words that will carry thinking the furthest. Many writers summarize the general purpose or main concepts from a source but then quote a key sentence or phrase that best characterizes the ideas. Big insights come as a result of **strategic quotation**.*

Finally, a good summary, paraphrase, and quotation rely on a deep understanding of the source. When writers *get* a book, article, or blog, they know the nuances, the critical insights, and the reasons the source matters. So the best thing writers can do when it comes to summary, paraphrase, and quotation is to know their sources! That means reading closely and repeatedly. It also means trying to understand the original audience for the source, the debates or tensions surrounding the source, and the purpose of the writer. In short, read for context.

Activity Prompt: Choose one of the sources you found for the activity at the end of Applying a Supportive Source (earlier in this chapter). Then, (A) write a summary of the source, and (B) choose a key quotation that characterizes the source. In a small group, describe the source you chose and then read your summary and quotation aloud. How do others in your group understand your source based on your summary and selected quotation? Do they *get it*? If not, discuss how your summary or quotation can be further refined to capture the source's main point.

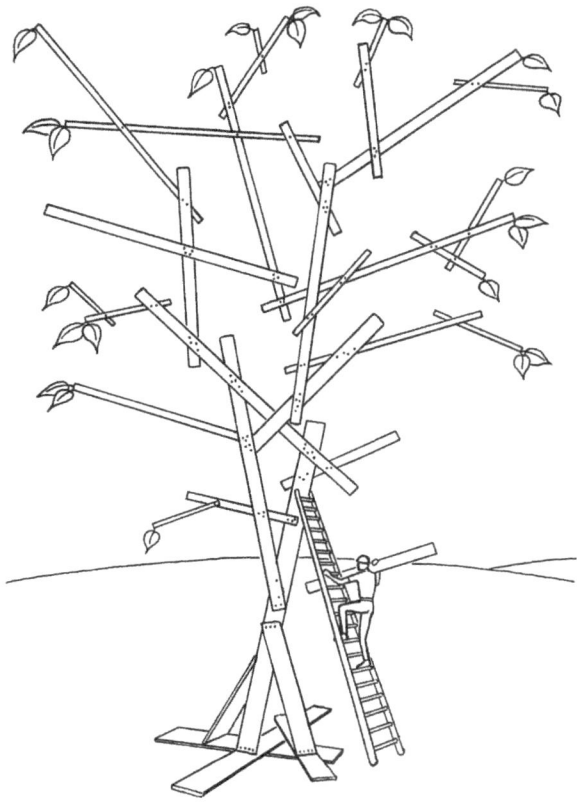

(3) Synthesizing Sources

Good writers can bring together, or *synthesize*, a range of supportive sources. They assemble several sources into one passage and integrate them to develop a point. For example, let's return to the topic of myth and modern life. The following passage brings two sources together: Joseph Campbell and screenwriter Christopher Vogler.

> As Joseph Campbell made clear, heroes—both ancient and modern—follow a path, one that can be witnessed in stories, novels, plays, legends, and modern film. That path includes a range of familiar steps. For instance, the hero must have some special origin or birth, not necessarily elevated but defined by

> *something out of the ordinary. The hero must also face early tests—challenges that hasten maturity or raise questions about the hero's roll in the world. The hero's story intensifies with a "call to adventure," a quest or mission that comes from some strange or outside force. And what's key, according to filmmaker and theorist Christopher Vogler, is the transition from the Ordinary World to the Special World. In taking on this new mission, the hero must cross a "threshold" into a different reality, one that requires a new level or awareness or skill or both.*

The passage applies two sources to round out an understanding of a complex idea. The sources do more than support a point. Throughout the paragraph, Campbell and Vogler's language builds an increasingly detailed way of thinking about the hero. In this case, the sources have similar, even overlapping, ways of describing the topic. In fact, Vogler, the second source, takes many ideas directly from Campbell. Using Vogler, then, is simply a matter of emphasis. He helps to shed additional light on part of Campbell's concepts.

But synthesis can also involve sources that disagree. That means writers may bring together opposing or conflicting sources—using them to show conflict and tension surrounding a topic. In fact, any given topic resounds with conflicting opinions, even outright debate. Often, the tension is spelled out for all to see. The parties involved argue openly over a point. Highlighting that disagreement can be a powerful move. For example, the following passage introduces a third source, one that partly disagrees with Campbell and Vogler. As writers, we can bring that dissenting source into the mix and even offer commentary of our own:

> *According to Simon Benlow, "Modern life requires that myths fade, that people look for meaning in their communities, in shared efforts, even scientific methodology. You can't cure cancer with a story—no matter how compelling—but with others who are doing the serious work of here-and-now." While Benlow makes an important point about community, he does not strike down Campbell's point. After all, modern heroes can be physicists, chemists, genealogists, philosophers, linguists. They can rely fully on the institutions of today but still follow an ancient path, a timeless pattern that brings them through their efforts.*

Here, the passage synthesizes sources that clearly disagree. But sometimes the tension among sources isn't as obvious. In fact, scholarship is full of gray areas. People agree, disagree, agree a little, and disagree a little. It's not simply a matter of black and white. There is a sliding range of positions:

Outright Disagreement (*Why They Are So Very Wrong*): Disagreement is sometimes dressed up in highly formal terms. Other times, it is as brazen as a political debate on cable news. Of course, it depends on the context: whether the disagreement takes place in an academic journal, a personal blog, or a conference presentation. (See "Considering the Context" in Chapter 3 for more on context.) Regardless of the context, good writers are careful not to target or condemn a particular person. Instead, they disagree with a position, policy, claim, or theory:

- The athletic department's approach misses the nature of the key problem.
- The school board's public statements contradict its own mission statements.
- The article incorrectly separates creative thinking from "higher order" thinking.

Qualified Disagreement (*Why They Are a Little Off*): Even when we find a flaw with a position, theory, or trend, we can still find some value in it. In other words, we can find a reason for not trashing it outright:

- While Keynesian economics helped governments weather the crises of the twentieth century, it missed the impact of foreign currencies.
- Although Lanham acknowledges the growth of Indian cinema, he ignores problems within the Indian economy.
- The proposed policy for genome research only goes so far.

Qualified Agreement (*Why They Almost Have It Right*): Even when we find value in someone else's position, we may still find some flaw—a shortcoming in the data, a misstep in the reasoning, a slight error in judgment. For example, physicists today acknowledge some flaws in Einstein's theories, but they also acknowledge his contributions to the field. In other words, it's okay to support, even to celebrate, a position and still point out a minor flaw:

- Smith is correct in one important aspect of the argument.
- Despite its minor problems, Smith's argument highlights some important layers of the writing process.

- Some new media theorists, especially those tuned into streaming technologies, have begun to consider an important dimension: the physical limitations of the human eye and brain.

Outright Agreement (*Why They Are So Very Right*): Despite all the suspicious minds and serious doubts, we sometimes agree entirely with someone else's position. In fact, we may even celebrate others' positions with absolute enthusiasm:

- Kenneth Burke's take on human motive moved the entire field of study into decades of important questions.
- Third-wave feminists generated the most powerful political insights of the era.

Good thinkers and writers acknowledge the range of positions in any debate and seek the nuances within those positions. As we make sense of sources, we should consider how they relate to one another within this spectrum of agreement.

Activity Prompt: One powerful strategy for understanding an article, book, or blog is to ask some basic questions about the underlying tension: Is there a debate about the issue? What is the nature of the debate? What are the positions? What names are associated with each position? Where does the author of this specific source come down? With whom does he or she agree and disagree? What is the nature of the agreement or disagreement? Apply these questions to sources you find for a current writing project.

Key Questions

Good writers don't ignore disagreements! In fact, they include some tension, some moments of friction, to show the complexity of a topic. After examining your sources, consider the following:

- How do my sources agree? What basic ideas do they share? When describing the issue or topic under consideration, what similar terms or phrases do they use? What values do they seem to share? What facts or information do they share?
- How do my sources disagree? When describing the issue or topic, what different terms or phrases do they use? What do those different

terms or phrases suggest about their positions? How might their values differ? How do they disagree about basic facts?

(4) Drawing from the Past

New information from sources can be valuable to writers. But we should not fall into the trap of currency. In other words, we should not believe that the best sources—the only usable sources—are those from the present. New information isn't *always* the best or even the most helpful. It depends largely on the nature of our writing project and the nature of our claims. If we're making a time-sensitive claim, then the newest, most recent source is great. If we're making a timeless claim or exploring an issue that extends over long periods (decades, centuries, millennia), then older sources may be quite helpful.

Time-Sensitive Claims

- The 2024 hurricane season is changing how Americans understand home insurance.
- AI is quickly changing how local school boards imagine high school curriculum.
- Pharmaceutical drug abuse is still a profound problem among teenagers.

Less Time-Sensitive Claims

- Hurricanes have traditionally prompted political discussions about disaster relief funds.
- AI will continue to impact educational policy.
- Drug abuse among teenagers includes a range of legal and illegal substances.

More Timeless Claims

- Natural disasters often prompt difficult national discussions about aid to victims.

- New technologies tend to shape educational policy in the short and long term.
- Adolescent rebellion often includes substance abuse.

The point here is that writers need not stay in the present. If our projects and claims allow, we can travel through time and assemble sources from different decades, centuries, and cultures. We don't have to keep our heads in one era or one location. We can make a connection between a new bit of data and a historic insight. (See "Make New Comparisons" in Chapter 1 for more on making connections among ideas.) The following passage relies on a historical idea. Even while focusing on a current issue—climate change—it borrows from the past, specifically, the words of President John F. Kennedy:

When calling for the US space program to head for the moon, President Kennedy argued we should take on missions "not because they are easy, but because they are hard." Reaching the moon seemed impossible at the time, a challenge far beyond our technological capabilities. But the challenge brought forward the best thinkers, the best inventors and problem solvers. When it comes to the climate crisis, the same can said today. Millions of people believe the climate issues are too big, too hard to manage. They believe that humans cannot possibly intervene in natural systems that transcend national borders and continents. But the challenge alone will call upon the most sophisticated researchers, the most committed and skilled problem solvers.

This move of reaching into the past can also be personal. In other words, writers can explain how they found an older source and what it means for their current thinking:

I was taught to respect other people's religious beliefs. No matter what I believe, my parents insisted that others' beliefs should not be degraded or dismissed. Because religion is so often part of a cultural tradition, an entire way of living in the world, it's dangerous or just foolish to stomp on an entire religious view. This basic degree of respect got bolstered recently when I encountered C.S. Lewis's works. In his book, **Abolition of Man***, he argues that all the world's major religions share basic principles, a universal set of beliefs about kindness, honor, and duties to others. These basic principles, which he simply calls the* **Tao***, reinforce a shared respect. If religions have so much in common, all believers must agree on countless basics. We may not live the same, vote the same, dress the same, but we likely want to live in a similar world.*

As these passages show, vital ideas are still waiting in the past. Positions and insights that have been buried by recent trends and general forgetfulness can still fortify our thinking. The best contemporary thinkers retrieve those insights and *pull them forward* into the present.

(5) Trusting but Verifying

Most writers and editors want to publish good information. They put their names on articles, books, and blogs and don't want their reputations tarnished because of something they've said or written. In other words, most people who write and publish—who create material we call a *source*—do not seek to misinform readers. While politicians, influencers, and media celebrities sometimes seek to misinform their audiences, most authors and editors are simply trying to publish helpful and interesting information. For this reason, we can research with the belief that other writers are doing their best, communicating reliable information, and putting forward opinions that can stand the test of time.

However, even well-intentioned people get things wrong. They accept information from another source (or many sources) that turns out to be false or incomplete. They repeat wrong numbers, inaccurate information, or incomplete reports without realizing it. Even trustworthy institutions can fall into this trap. In fact, it happens often enough that we should have sound strategies for distinguishing between good, questionable, and bad information.

Researchers often use the terms *reliable* or *unreliable* when it comes to sources. If information is reliable, it can be tracked down. Its origins are given or easily discovered. In real practice, many authors and editors try to signal reliability. They make simple but important moves to help us feel better about the information. They give names, dates, and publication information directly in their writing. Less worthy (and more questionable) sources do the opposite. For example, if an article about hurricanes gives specific information, it is more reliable if we can see where the information is from—who developed it, when, and under what circumstances. A less reliable article would simply give the information and leave us guessing where it's from. Consider the following examples. The first list shows some conventional strategies for helping us see the reliability of information. The second list shows how authors can sometimes hide the sources of information:

More Reliable

- According to Michael Brennan, director of the National Hurricane Center . . .
- A report published in November 2024 by the Pew Research Center . . .
- The *Washington Post* editorial board made its case in an October op-ed . . .

Less Reliable

- Many people now believe . . .
- According to the latest research . . .
- Various sources have concluded . . .

For all these reasons, reliable sources *attribute*, and it's the main reason teachers always want writers to *cite* their sources. (See the next section in this chapter.) Giving detailed information about one's sources is the single best way to signal reliability. In other words, when writers cite and document sources, they are saying, in effect, "here's where I found all my information and here's where you can check it for yourself!" The most reliable sources even contextualize reference information. In other words, they explain how and where studies or experiments were carried out. When we read such sources, we know instantly where all the information is coming from and how it was developed.

More Reliable

- Information can be tracked.
- Sources are named, cited, or attributed.
- Studies or reports are contextualized.
- The research process is made clear.

Less Reliable

- Information cannot be tracked.
- Sources are nameless or generalized.
- Studies or reports are mentioned but not contextualized.
- The writer does not explain research methods.

Finally, there's another, broader issue to consider when it comes to sources, and it relates to the general way knowledge develops through time. In all fields of study, experts work to get things right. They try to make history, biology, physics, psychology, and so on more accurate. That means they discover problems with the past and present. They realize that other scholars may have been wrong and then try to redirect attention to some better way of thinking. And sometimes, that process—of trying to get things right—can even create errors! Experts are human. And humans make mistakes.

(6) Citing Sources

Once we start using sources, we enter an important and long-standing tradition of citing those sources. The process involves *attributing* information to specific sources and telling your readers how to track down those sources if they choose. As the previous section explains, this simply means that we should connect specific information to a specific source. Depending on the audience and situation, this process can range from informal (giving a name in a sentence) to formal (documenting the author, date of publication, publication type, permanent URL). The important point is to identify the source in a way that corresponds to your readers' expectations and feels appropriate for your project.

The Long Buildup: Sometimes, writers take several sentences to introduce and contextualize a source. They explain the source's credentials, background, or influence in the field before they integrate relevant ideas. This is usually the case when writers are drawing from a vital source—one that has a big impact on the project's ideas:

> When it comes to Hollywood movies and the role of mythology, Christopher Vogler has been a major influence. In 1992, he wrote a lengthy memo that explained Joseph Campbell's understanding of myth so that screenwriters could better shape stories for the big screen. The memo had huge impact on Hollywood—on the way people crafted plots, main characters, and scenes. In **The Writer's Journey: Mythic Structure for Writers**, Vogler lays out the basics of mythological and modern movie heroes. He argues, like Campbell, that the hero's journey is universal—therefore experienced by all (4).

The Quick Tag: If a source isn't necessarily vital—if it's simply providing support or expressing a position in a debate—writers often give a quick tag. In other words, they don't give background information about that source. They simply set up the idea, relay the information (in a summary, paraphrase, or quotation), and then cite it. For example, if we needed a quick fact about movie trends, we wouldn't need to give background on our source. We could simply attribute the information, quote the language, and move on:

> *Streaming has increased viewers' ability to binge watch old and new programs alike. Adweek claims that 40% of people binge for multiple hours.*

In magazines, newspapers, and blogs, writers credit their sources using one of the two strategies above. In other words, they give a name and a title if appropriate. Occasionally, they may also tell when the source was published. But in academic work and longer book-length projects, writers must always give complete information: page numbers, publisher information, and publication dates. And that's where specific formatting comes in— where formal documentation styles are used so that readers can trace the information if they choose. The documentation styles differ depending on the academic field and the publication.

The first passage above (about Vogler) uses a numerical reference. The (4) at the end of the passage refers to the page number in Vogler's book that contains the information. Because the passage follows the rules established by the Modern Language Association (MLA), it references the page number. The final page of the essay would give all the publication information in a Works Cited or References list:

> *Jones, Chris. "Christopher Vogler and the Hero's Journey: The Outline, the Archetypes, and the Mythical Memo." 22 September 2024, https://chrisjonesblog.com/ 10 October 2024.*

Activity Prompt: If you're writing a formal project for a college course, don't just guess at the process of citing sources. As you may know, not all disciplines (not even all professors in each discipline) follow the same rules for citing sources. Most college writing-intensive courses slot time for learning the rules of a particular documentation style, such as Modern Language Association (MLA) or American Psychological Association (APA) style. Before you get too involved in citation, it may be valuable to ask which style is most preferred.

Writing Prompts

Sources help to shake up our ideas and get us thinking in new ways. But it takes some work to find sources that are useful and to weave the ideas from those sources into your own writing. As you consider your own project, take one of the following paths:

1. Think about the present condition or state of a particular practice like Facebooking or a public trend like voting among eighteen-year-olds. Do some online research on your topic and find out what others are saying about it. Try to find the thoughts of both average people and scholars in the most relevant discipline (communications or cultural studies). In an essay, describe the trend and use the moves from this chapter: apply a supportive source, draw from a vital source, and synthesize. Develop a thesis about your topic that takes various viewpoints into account. Keep going back to your sources, letting them inform each new idea you develop. Search for insights in your sources and apply them, in the form of summary, quotation, or paraphrase, as you develop your points. (Cite sources according to the documentation style your instructor specifies.)

2. Choose a current tension or conflict in a field of study. For example, if you're interested in nursing, you might consider the debate surrounding hospital versus hospice care. Or if you're interested in economics, you might focus on arguments about the future of the euro. In an essay, detail the nature of the tension and the positions that have developed around it. How many positions can you identify? Who represents each position? When did the debate begin, and how has it changed over time? Do the different sides agree about anything? What insights emerge from examining these different voices alongside one another?

6 Seeking Tension

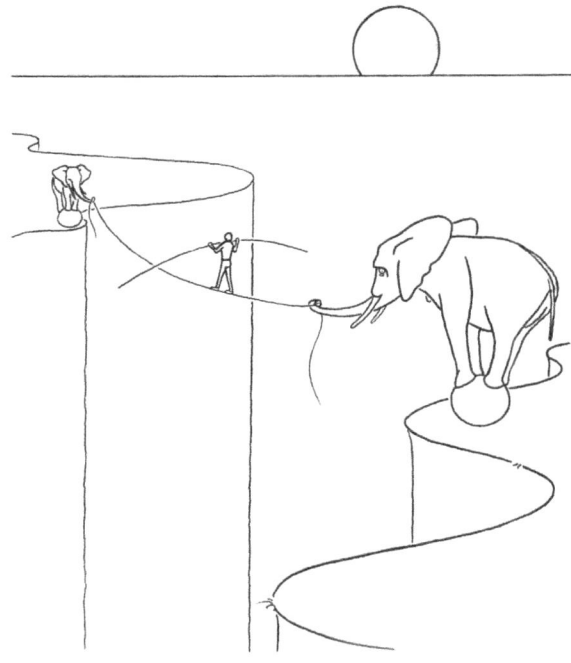

In daily life, most people do their best to avoid conflict. By and large, we steer clear of open debate and outright tension. We don't *usually* jump out of our cars and accost bad drivers. We don't grab strangers' cell phones and hang them up if they're talking too loudly. We live and let live when it comes to most public situations. In fact, psychologists claim that a healthy state of mind depends, in part, on our ability to let many potential conflicts pass us by. Otherwise, we'd get caught up in nonstop friction. But when it comes to smart writing, tension is unavoidable. In fact, good writers and thinkers go looking for it. They focus on disagreement and debate. They also seek out quieter forms of tension: uncertainty, intellectual gaps, and cracks in meaning. In short, if there's something slightly wrong or unresolved, good writers seize on it.

Young writers need help with this skill. They need help recognizing the value of tension—what it is, what it does for an intellectual task. After all, much formal schooling involves *solving* problems and moving on. Students learn to tie up loose ends (or ignore them), and because they've been prompted from their earliest years to solve, they've often learned to avoid brambles that might seem unsolvable. Therefore, they may be surprised to know that intellectual tension can serve them. They might be startled to know that tension is often good.

In short, this chapter can be a revelation to students. If they can begin to understand the intellectual value of tension, teachers can make significant inroads. While the first chapter focuses on strategies for seeking complexity, the strategies here are closely related. Tension, after all, is a kind of complexity. But it's so important that it warrants its own examination. This chapter offers three moves: (1) detecting subtle tension, (2) connecting to broad tensions, (3) breaking up dualities.

(1) Detecting Subtle Tension

Open conflict is easy to see. It involves physical standoffs, vocal debate, and obvious pressure. It's the thing that drives action movies. It's the energy that generates political debates, hallway fights, and family disputes. In open conflict, the parties usually understand the point of disagreement: the buried treasure is mine, not yours; the tax code benefits the rich, not the middle class; you spilled grape soda on my boots; and so on. But subtle tension moves along quietly. It lurks in corners. And you don't have to be a scholar to know when it's there. Whenever a situation doesn't conform to expectations, or vice versa, we experience some intellectual friction, some quiet discomfort. That discomfort is powerful. It's a writer's tool. In fact, the gap between writers' expectations and their actual discoveries (what they see, hear, detect, read) can be a creative element.

Imagine a high school senior, Katherine, who is visiting college campuses. As part of her visits, she attends a sophomore-level English course that does not conform to her thinking. In the following passage, she describes her own surprise:

> *As I sat through English 267, I witnessed the opposite of nearly all my own classes. Through years of elementary, middle, and high school, I sat along with other students, usually in rows, while a teacher stood or sat at the front of class*

either watching over us or addressing us all. Sometimes, students would break into working groups while the teacher would circulate through the room. But in English 267, a course focused on social media and public identity, students were basically on their own. The professor gave a few brief announcements at the start, and then students met with previously assigned groups. They didn't dally, gab, or anything that might be called off-task. Granted, there was an occasional laugh, a joke here or there, but the groups had a mission, something they'd been assigned to accomplish over several weeks, and they were determined to achieve it. Here were students only two or three years older than me and my classmates, and they had a totally different approach to education. They oversaw their own work and knew they wouldn't get direct feedback for weeks. They even charted out assignments within their own groups—who was responsible for what—so they were accountable to one another, not necessarily the professor. It was this self-accountability that struck me most, something that high school students must, at some point, acquire if they are to succeed at college or anywhere beyond senior year.

Katherine had some well-established notions of school, but she witnessed the opposite. The events didn't line up with her expectations, and that *misalignment* provoked thinking. In her writing, she does not discount the experience, nor does she ignore or dismiss her own sense of wonder. Instead, she explains the gap between her observation and her assumptions.

Like Katherine, good writers and thinkers can consider the misalignment between what we see and what we expect. We can have an open mind—not open to *any* idea that comes rolling along, but open to investigating situations that don't immediately line up with our assumptions. We can try to understand *why* things don't conform. And perhaps most importantly, we shouldn't lunge for a quick resolution. We shouldn't hope to end the friction but to study it.

This intellectual impulse may sound rather sophisticated, but it's not out of reach, not even close. In fact, the first move is easy to comprehend. It simply involves recognizing one's own discomfort or surprise. If we are struggling to make sense of something, our first thought might be something like, "Well, this is weird." That weirdness, that sense that something is a little off, can be an important opportunity. In short, if we sense something slightly askew—a little off—that's half the battle. From there, we can think through that feeling.

In the following passages, the writer describes a surprising idea—something that doesn't make automatic sense. Then the writer *begins* exploring the gap between expectations and reality. In other words, these passages show how writers start exploring the gap between expectations and experience.

Personal Narrative

Last year, when I first entered science class, I expected a straight-forward introduction to biology. Like my peers, I assumed we'd hear a brief lecture on biology itself and what we'd be doing to get a grip on the basics. My understanding of class introductions came from years of first days—those initial meetings when teachers chart out a path, state some rules of the road, and hand out materials. Because it was a science class, I also expected some dry information. Instead, Mr. Walsh began with a lengthy poem about nature. Along with the other students, I sat wondering if I'd come to the right room, if I'd somehow lost track of my schedule.

As the hour continued, Mr. Walsh argued that science was, at its heart, about wonder. Biology, he said, asks nonstop questions about the nature of life itself. When one question gets answered, another comes along, then another, and so on. The process of seeking answers is science but so is the impulse to ask basic questions. In some respects, this made good sense, but I still didn't understand—at that point—how my appreciation or understanding of a poem would help me get into the particulars of a science course.

Informative/Argumentative

Superhero movies have dominated theaters for years. At their peak, in 2023, according to The Numbers, superhero movies accounted for more than 30% of all tickets sold. Most of these titles, including Marvel franchises, feature fierce and determined heroes, figures who battle an evil force threatening all of humanity. While they may struggle with personal demons of their own, they remain calm and collected. They don't mess around or pull pranks. They're superheroes after all! They have a world to save. Enter Deadpool.

With three popular movies, Deadpool's success doesn't make much sense. He's a clown who refuses to take himself or his enemies seriously. Unlike most every other hero (from Batman to Captain Marvel to Black Panther), Deadpool makes nonstop jokes even while battling his greatest foes. He's so completely different from the dark, brooding, serious superhero. Even his injuries are funny.

He gets squashed, cut, shot, severed, and each time, the scene draws attention to the weirdness of his problem—not the apparent pain or danger of such injuries. In this sense, Deadpool movies are straight-up comedies. So why do they work? What draws millions of viewers?

Activity Prompt: Good writers pounce on moments of wonder or strangeness. They pause and study the gap between what they've assumed and what they're witnessing. In a small group, discuss a situation in which one or more of you experienced a gap between your expectations and your observation. In other words, if any of you thought, "well, this is weird," discuss the situation. What didn't make sense? Why? How did you respond? What questions did the situation provoke? What feelings did it provoke? Finally, why didn't the situation make sense at first? Or why might it continue to seem strange?

Key Questions

- What's typical here? What's supposed to happen?
- What's really happening?
- What are the differences between expectations and reality?
- What do those differences show about our expectations?

(2) Connecting to a Broader Tension

Good writers find patterns. They imagine how individual moments connect across time and space, even how ideas from different contexts might relate to each other. The same goes for tension. Good writers try to understand how a particular misalignment or confusion relates to something broader—to some friction that extends beyond the moment. For example, in the classroom scenario above (where a student hears a poem on the first day of biology), students would start by trying to understand what they were supposed to do. But as they thought through the situation, they might also consider some broader tensions related to learning, school, motivation, and uncertainty. They might, for instance, think about the difference between active and passive learning, students and consumers, or even learning and unlearning. In other words, they might connect their particular situation to a bigger and more long-standing issue.

In her writing, mentioned above, Katherine makes such a connection. At the outset, she seizes on a specific tension between her expectations and what she observed:

- What She Expected: Students learn material directly from a professor.
- What She Witnessed: Students were developing their own material without the professor's direct oversight.

She does more than simply note the difference between high school and college—or at least this particular college classroom. She studies it and discovers something she calls *self-accountability*. She could, then, explore the broader tension between high school and college education—and the whole set of behaviors that accompany students as they make that transition.

The following passages take up topics from the previous section and connect the initial tension to a broader issue. In other words, the writers here link the specific tension (about poetry in a science class or a superhero's unconventional nature) to a longstanding friction.

Personal Narrative

*When schools separate different subjects into different classrooms, they also divide students' understanding of the world. We are taught that science belongs **over here**, language study **over there**, numbers in yet another place. We learn to see our own study in neat categories—like cafeteria trays with little rectangular boxes for each food item. We're sometimes even told that different studies correspond to certain parts of the brain. From there, teachers, parents, counselors, and academic advisors explain that people are wired for one subject more than others. In other words, the whole system encourages us to see absolute division between subjects. We are taught in countless ways that science and poetry, for instance, are naturally distinct. But what's the point of these divisions? What do these categories do for us? Might learning poetry alongside biology—in the same course, in the same room with the same teacher—do something valuable for us?*

Informative/Argumentative

The Deadpool character fits into a long tradition: the unlikely hero, someone who doesn't want to save the world but does anyway. While not the same in appearance, Deadpool is like the Hobbits of Tolkien's **Lord of the Rings**. *Hobbits are humble, talkative, sometimes laughable halflings who save Middle Earth from Sauron's wrath. They are not mighty warriors but mild-mannered tinkerers. Of course, there are differences between them and Deadpool—who is, after all, a fierce opponent with a slew of weapons. But they are the same in one major way: they don't fit the traditional hero mold. Hobbits and Deadpool alike don't see themselves as heroes. In typical terms, they have no business saving the world or defeating its greatest enemy, and that is the essence of their appeal.*

Activity Prompt: In a small group, return to the classroom scenario—where the science teacher is reciting poetry. Connect that situation to the tension between active and passive learning. To do this, you might first try to describe active learning and passive learning. Make a list of the characteristics or behaviors you associate with each phrase, or search for each phrase online. Discuss how these characteristics relate to the classroom scenario.

(3) Advanced Move: Breaking Up Dualities

So far, this chapter has argued that writers can sense tension and examine it. In other words, all writers can, and should, study intellectual friction. This final section focuses on a particular type of tension known as *duality*, an opposing pair of ideas, for example:

- black/white
- up/down
- in/out
- us/them
- republican/democrat
- hate/love
- cause/effect
- before/after
- capitalism/socialism
- tyranny/democracy
- hot/cold

- powerful/powerless
- predator/prey
- beautiful/ugly
- opinion/fact

Such dualities, and many more, live in language. They make us think in particular ways—not all of them bad. For instance, it's helpful to see that tyranny and democracy are opposites: tyranny operates from the top down. It involves a few people, or one person, holding all political power and forcing it onto the masses. On the other hand, democracy enables the masses to determine how power will work. It's an important distinction that helps millions of people throughout the world understand their role in the social order.

However, dualities can bully our brains. They can gather in our thoughts and make us imagine two, and *only* two, contrary possibilities. In short, they can create *dualistic thinking*—an inability to see gray areas. When people fall prey to dualistic thinking, they see topics split down the middle. They see all paths as forked—one branch going left, the other going right. They fail to imagine multiple paths, many lines, or no lines at all. For example, consider the biology class example in the previous section: a science teacher using poetry for his opening lecture. An attentive writer might sense some dualistic thinking at work. On one hand, we have science, on another we have poetry, an art form. (Please see the following Sample Passages section for a way to break up that duality.)

Or consider the tyranny/democracy duality. At first glance, the two forms of government seem absolutely distinct. And in many ways, they are: In tyranny, the masses are controlled by a single leader. In democracy, policies are determined by a majority of voters. But if we can think beyond the duality, we might see some gray areas. Here's one example: In the early nineteenth century, the French scholar Alexis de Tocqueville cautioned against a "tyranny of the majority"—the power of many people to squash the hopes of a minority. Democracy, he explained, is not free of tyranny. If given absolute rule, a majority can enact the same degree of terror and oppression as a forceful king. If we cannot imagine this possibility (if we believe that a majority *always* acts democratically), we may not ask some crucial policy questions. We may even be blind to big problems.

The point here is that we don't always have to choose A or B, science or art, tyranny or democracy, on or off, family or community. There's no overarching rule that says we *must* think in dualities. Often, in fact, dualities keep us from understanding the complexity of an issue. And while thinking beyond dualism can be a challenge, all writers can definitely do it!

Many writers set up a duality by explaining two opposing ideas and the friction between them. After that explanation, they run up the middle and show the gray area in between. In the first passages below, the opposing ideas are entrenched in our conversations about ourselves and others. The first sample passage points out the science/art duality but also hints at the intellectual problems that come from it. The second takes on human/nature duality, and the third takes up the Marvel Comics hero brought up earlier in this chapter:

Science/Art: My family tends to think of itself as scientific. My parents and siblings all make clear that they are science-oriented in nature and that they're better off leaving art to someone else. They believe in this distinction: science is one thing, art something else entirely. But as we've learned in biology, science has wonder at its root. Similarly, all artforms work from a sense of wonder, from a desire to see or express something mysterious in the world or the human condition. Also, as any poet, photographer, or musician will explain, art requires intense focus on rules. It's not a free-for-all. Artists in all fields study the procedures, conventions, and exact steps for developing their craft. Of course, they may "draw outside the lines," but the best artists in any field, know the lines very well.

Human/Nature: We are often taught to see nature as a realm of harmony or balance while humans, on the other hand, are cast as inherently destructive. In this perspective, nature somehow sustains itself and its only enemy is the brutal impulse of humans. But this is dangerous dualism. As it turns out, nature is terrifically destructive—not just to buildings, bridges, and roads. It's destructive to animals, plants, and habitat. Fire, floods, wind, extreme heat, punishing cold can all ravage ecosystems. Animals are constantly fleeing nature's own hand. And while human developments have certainly destroyed countless habitats and eradicated millions of species, humans have also nurtured natural habitats for thousands of years. Through farming, careful planning, and a range of preservation efforts, humans have worked to keep nature alive.

Sometimes, those efforts are hard to see, even harder to acknowledge, they are real and dramatic.

Clown/Hero: With its third installment, the Deadpool franchise now fits into a longstanding trend: the buddy story. In this film category, an unlikely duo forms, one clownish and talkative, the other serious and brooding. The pattern was established decades ago with programs such as **The Odd Couple** *or even with comedy teams like Abbott and Costello. The crime fighting duo became well established through a long list of films:* **48 Hours, Lethal Weapon, Rush Hour, Pulp Fiction, Hot Fuzz,** *and so on. And the latest Deadpool film borrows from that history. Deadpool himself remains the talkative but effective buffoon while Wolverine wears usual scowl. Together, the two crime fighters embody the old tension. Audiences, then, can have the clownish anti-hero and the self-possessed silent hero.*

Activity Prompts: If we are to think well, then we must break up dualities and escape the fog of bad thinking around them. Some of our worst thinking, in fact, happens when we allow common dualities to thrive, to bully us, and to make us blind to the gray areas. Once people fall on one side or the other, they often accept a huge list of beliefs that oppose the other side. The duality, then, creates a list of other dualities. Like intellectual demons, they take over and start reproducing in our heads.

1. Consider the conservative/liberal duality. As a group, list some beliefs that you think fit under each label. You might list beliefs according to specific topics such as taxes, the environment, poverty, LGBTQ rights, privacy, and gun laws. Consider one of these specific topics and try to discover a gray area. Beneath the obvious tension between liberals and conservatives, what beliefs might they share?
2. Examine the man/woman duality. What behaviors and descriptions keep the duality in place? What common phrases keep people from seeing the gray areas between men and women?

Writing Prompts

Good thinkers sense subtle tension. They consider what it means, how it works, why it's there in the first place. They seek it out, seize it, and develop insights before they even begin reaching for solutions. They embrace friction, study it, and even dissolve it from the inside out. Consider one of the following paths:

1. Attend a public concert, reading, or sporting event—one that you wouldn't normally be inclined to attend. Seek tension in the situation. Carefully monitor the behavior patterns you observe. Consider any action that seems out of sync with your expectations. Avoid judging the action. Instead, focus on the *misalignment* between what you're seeing and what you'd expect to see. Pursue that misalignment! What forces, reflexes, or policies might cause behaviors not to conform to your expectations?
2. Recall your first day of high school or work. Record your initial impressions—what you encountered, what you witnessed. What particular intellectual friction did you experience? After you describe that friction, launch outward to a broader tension. Connect to a long-standing cultural, economic, or philosophical tension.
3. Describe a specific event at your school or in your town. Explain what makes the event important to fellow students or citizens. Explain the shared understanding and any different or competing opinions about the event. What are the different ways of thinking about the event? How is the meaning or significance of the event quietly disputed? Does that quiet dispute relate to a broader cultural, educational, economic, physical, emotional, or even spiritual tension?

7 Inspecting the Terms

Language is alive. It morphs over time. New terms and phrases are constantly coming along while plenty of others fall out of favor or fade from common use. Consider these gems from the past: *knickers, house shoes, chap, davenport, galoshes, hullaballoo, scallywag, scurryfunge*. Terms like these have gone—or are going—extinct. Social and cultural forces are nudging them out of common use. This is not new. It's how language works. New products, new sensitivities, new trends, and new groups of people come along and influence language use. Slowly, and sometimes quickly, common terms fade. Not long ago, women were *dames*, men were *dudes*, money was *jack*, bling was an *orchid*, detectives were *dicks*, and great was *ducky*. Anyone who's lived more than a couple of decades can probably recall various substitutions. Language moves along at the speed of social life. Even though younger students haven't experienced such changes, they can still understand the process itself, and as writers, they can gain confidence as they inspect the terms within any given issue.

For students heading off to college, this phenomenon is especially important. Academic disciplines are ground zero for terminology flux. Terms fade because new tools replace old ones, new people enter the conversation, and new ideas become attractive. And in academic life, the process is often public and formal. Terms and phrases get examined in professional journals and at conferences. They get inspected, analyzed, and sometimes kicked to the sidelines. In fact, we might even say that academic terms don't simply fall out of fashion. Instead, they get kicked out of fashion! It all begins when someone detects something wrong:

- A term or phrase suggests an old prejudice, one not in keeping with current values.
- A term or phrase ignores complexity that should be considered.
- A term or phrase suggests something different from the normal activity or concept that writers want to engage.
- A term or phrase has gathered some negative, and therefore distracting, connotations.

For writers and researchers in academia, this is all serious business because the disciplines rely on key terms—those that show up in experiments, articles, books, and studies. The terms frame debates, make issues, and define the nature of study. Consider, for instance, the role of *consciousness* in psychology, *divine* in religion, *institution* in political science, or *voice* in literary studies. Academic writers rely on such terms in their own work, and if those terms get questioned or pushed aside, then the intellectual fabric of the discipline can change—maybe drastically. The hope, however, is that changes in the common terminology make for better thinking, better study, better research. Academic writers see this process as crucial—as part of their responsibility. They often set out to find gaps, old biases, or subtle inaccuracies in the language of the discipline.

This chapter focuses on that process and the following key moves: (1) detecting inaccuracy, (2) detecting quiet associations, (3) proposing a different term—one that's more accurate, (4) flipping the terms, (5) changing the lens. The moves in this chapter are argumentative in nature. They require writers to see a need for change, propose a change in terminology, and justify that change. Along the way, students might borrow some moves from Chapter 3, Analyzing Arguments or Chapter 4, Justifying a Position.

(1) Detecting Inaccuracy

When it comes to describing or explaining something, accuracy might not seem like a big deal. After all, an airplane will not fall from the sky if we use the wrong term. But the wrong term can do plenty of damage. It might hamper thinking. It might distort a clear picture or blur subtleties. And when writers are blind to subtleties, entire intellectual traditions can get bogged down or even travel along flawed paths for decades. So it's often up to individuals to make a case against terms—to call them out and describe the mental error they generate. For example, the following passage tackles a common word related to art:

> People often talk about art as a form expression. Whether painting, photography, music, poetry, or a whole new realm of digital manipulation, individual works get characterized as an artist's personal expression. Critics may say that a piece expresses something about the artist's life or the artist's understanding of the world. It's a common reflex to put **art** and **expression** together. Unfortunately, art has little to do with expression, and its typical association with art distorts what artists do and what great artists constantly work against.
>
> Expression comes from the Latin, meaning "to press out." When someone expresses juice from an orange, they squeeze what was locked within the rind. And when we use **express** to describe an artistic process or work, we suggest that the art itself was locked inside the person. But anyone who has worked tirelessly on a single piece of art or within a complicated field like music knows the opposite is true. A songwriter, for instance, spends years learning chord structure, melody, arrangement, even ensemble and recording techniques. None of these lurk quietly within a person. They are complex traditions that individual songwriters study. They acquire skills. They practice. They build a song, revise it, and rebuild parts using the shared chord patterns that millions of others have used. The song is not within the writer. Instead, it emerges from

the writer's interaction with an entire tradition—its tools, its conventions, its forms and formats, its technologies, and its contributors.

*When teachers, critics, sometimes artists themselves pair **art** and **expression**, they are following another tradition, one that ignores how art functions, one that ignores the immense amount of skill that great artists develop. Most importantly, the pairing of art and expression mis-educates young artists who are especially vulnerable to myths. Young artists might learn the exact wrong thing when it comes to making art. If they believe in expression, above and beyond all else, they won't lean fully into the necessary processes of revision. They won't bother to learn the subtleties of a tradition. They will even blame themselves—something deep within their own impulses—when a piece doesn't quite work out.*

This passage illustrates a common move among writers: they explain how a term distorts or misses something. In this sense, they are discovering more than a language problem. They are pointing out an intellectual flaw, a crisis in the shared thinking of the discipline.

Activity Prompt: Consider a common term or phrase related to school, such as *higher education, standardized test, unit, chapter test, midterm review,* or *knowledge retention*. How does the term or phrase miss something critical?

Key Question

What common term or phrase misses a real process or distorts what actually happens?

(2) Detecting Quiet Associations

Chapter One describes the way words come along with a string of quiet associations. For example, when most people see the phrase *high school,* they think of teachers, hallways, books, maybe a sport or marching band. Language works because people share in these associations. But sometimes, it's this layer—the unspoken layer—that creates problems. For example, a famous anthropologist, Margaret Mead, once detected something amiss with *superstition* and the way the term gets used in cultural anthropology. When researchers refer to a culture's beliefs as *superstitious*, according to Mead, they unknowingly dismiss those beliefs as less worthy of study, less worthy of serious examination. Mead was not saying that researchers purposely use *superstition* to insult the beliefs of other people. Instead, she was explaining that the term has some quiet associations that work against research. It's the quiet thinking—the intellectual stuff that rolls in on the coattails of the term—that Mead wanted her audience to consider.

Let's look more closely at the term *superstition*: why might the term pose problems for anthropologists—researchers who seek to understand civilization and human relations? To answer this, we should consider the way people commonly use the term. In mainstream American culture, superstition includes fear of broken mirrors, the number 13, Friday the 13th, black cats crossing one's path, and so on. Imagine that an office manager, let's call him Mark, refuses to leave home on Friday the 13th. Despite important meetings and deadlines, he insists that going out for any reason on that day poses serious danger. Although he can't prove it, Mark believes in some cause/effect relationship between the designation of the day and the potential for harm. His coworkers would probably wonder about his mental stability. They would call him superstitious. Let's say that another office manager, Leah, decides to stay home and crouched in her basement because a tornado is bearing down on the city. We wouldn't call her superstitious. We'd call her sane, normal, even responsible.

So people assign the term *superstition* to Marks of the world, not Leahs of the world. In its most common use, *superstition* refers to beliefs that are commonly dismissed as quaint or exotic—as less in touch with cause and effect, less reasonable, less scientific, less enlightened. So if anthropologists refer to another culture's beliefs as *superstition*, they automatically (but quietly) portray that culture as less reasonable, less intelligent. In short, they make a subtle judgment about the culture by simply assigning the term. Mead, then, drew attention to that subtle judgment and explained how it infects anthropologists' thinking.

Mead's move is not unique. Many writers deal with quiet associations. They probe the realm of attitudes, beliefs, and sentiments that linger around terms. The following passage continues inspecting the pairing of art and expression (introduced in the previous section):

> When someone uses a common phrase, we call it "an expression." For instance, a friend recently said he was "shooting for tomorrow" when asked

*about getting back to school from an illness. Someone challenged his use of **shooting**, saying that the term brings up some bad thoughts about guns. In response, my friend simply said, "Hey, it's just an expression." Whenever people say this—"it's just expression"—they mean it's an automatic response, something without intent. The expresser isn't carefully crafting a point but merely tossing out some preformed language. This common usage shows, in some respects, how mainstream culture thinks about art: it's not a conscious, thoughtful, and carefully planned process. It's just something that happens. But real artists know the truth. Ultimately, they must abandon the mainstream usage and learn how art really works.*

Such a strategy calls out the usual associations and inaccuracies that come along with words and phrases. The terms they target can be obstacles to better thinking or distractions to better questions. And it's those obstacles and distractions that academic writers want to omit.

Activity Prompt: As a class or group, examine another term and consider its quiet associations, the automatic ideas that come with the term itself. Consider, for instance, one of the following: *ethnic, third world, mature, punk, book-smart, hot*. List the associations that come to mind. Also discuss how the situation, or context, might affect the associations of the term.

Key Question

Focus on a common term or phrase related to your writing topic. What are the quiet associations? For instance, what notions of right, wrong, good, bad, powerful, or weak come along with the term or phrase?

(3) Proposing a Different Term

Once an old term is shown to be flawed, there's room to offer something different. Sometimes writers propose a substitution—something more accurate or something with less cultural baggage. For example, the following passage proposes a new term (and metaphor) to replace *expression* in art. The new terms more appropriately describe how art gets made:

*Artists do anything but express, so teachers and critics (anyone who discusses art publicly) should throw the term out the window. Instead, they should try other terms, those that help to characterize artistic processes. Artists **build, invent, shape, formulate, conjure,** and **craft**. In fact, I believe the final term, **craft**, suggests the real commitment of artists. It gets close to the self-conscious processes of developing a complex work, the countless decisions and revisions that occur at each moment. It also carries with it the suggestion of history. In its noun form, craft refers to a tradition. People learn a craft. They study what others have done, how others succeeded, how others failed and tried again.*

When language around art changes, artists will more quickly get beyond the myths, the unhelpful baggage related to their chosen fields. They'll get over the bad—sometimes disastrous—impulse to celebrate or condemn something deep within themselves. Young artists will be healthier, more studious, and less self-involved.

Sometimes, the change in terms is a shift away from an entire worldview. The writer introduces a new linguistic creature that takes up residence in everyday talk. We see such creation all the time when it comes to technology. Years ago, *Facebook* had no meaning whatsoever—nor did *blog, Wi-Fi,* or *nanotechnology*. Now those terms are widely used. New situations also generate new terms or acronyms that function like words:

He got Me-Too-ed.
The MAGA crowd cheered her ideas.
Katy Perry dropped her new single to less-than-stellar reviews.

And sometimes writers create new terms to accompany and cultivate a new way of thinking. They offer something totally distinct to help people get beyond the status quo—or the usual ways of thinking. (Also see Chapter 8, Escape the Status Quo, which explores this move in depth.)

Activity Prompt: In a small group, take on the issue of people pairing *expression* and *art*. A previous passage proposes that artists should use *craft* instead of *express*: *The artist crafted her message through sculpture.* But consider some other term, something completely fresh. Go outside of art itself. Consider other walks of life: agriculture, politics, military, space travel, technology, environmental studies, neurology, and so on. Borrow a term from one of these other fields and propose it as a new way to describe artistic work.

Key Questions

- How could a new term better describe the action, condition, or thing under consideration?
- What other walks of life or academic disciplines might contribute a helpful term?
- What term might you create (or coin) to better capture the action, condition, or thing under consideration?

(4) Advanced Move: Flipping the Terms

Sometimes, the most powerful way to change terms is to flip them upside down, to invert the logic that lurks within them so that *doing* becomes *undoing*, *destruction* becomes *creation*, *seeing* becomes *blindness*, *multiplying* becomes *dividing*, and on and on. One famous version of this is the statement: "A way of seeing is also a way of not seeing." In other words, developing a perspective means developing a blindness to things outside of that perspective. A less formal version of this has been popularized and spread around on bumper stickers: "Don't Believe Everything You Think."

The process is not simply a thought experiment; it is an intellectual maneuver to open up possibilities. It may sound difficult—and it can be—but it happens all the time in daily life, even in informal conversations. As we're talking, we suddenly understand that the opposite of what we've said, or were going to say, makes more sense. In other words, the opposite of our normal intellectual path can sometimes create insights. For instance, humanities scholar Robert Bringhurst once flipped some common thinking about poetry by explaining that words are made of poetry, rather than the opposite. He was insisting that poetry is something before or beyond words—the inverse of what people normally think. Like Margaret Mead, Robert Bringhurst shows how thinking gets caged in a common and uninspected phrase. In fact, plenty of creative writers have put their brains in a kind of inverse relationship with common ways of thinking. They've imagined the opposite, the inside/out or the upside/down of the usual. History is filled with their eye-opening ideas:

- Jane Goodall argued that studying chimpanzees could show us something crucial about humans.
- Adam Gopnik argued that dogs have figured out what it means to be human, while humans still don't understand what it means to be a dog.
- Michael Pollan claimed that plants like potatoes and apples have used humans to thrive—rather than the opposite.

Activity Prompt: In a small group, take on a common term related to writing, such as *inspire, express, convince, develop,* or *edit*. After you choose a term, imagine its opposite. How might the opposite term say something about the process of writing? Might the opposite reveal something important? Can you imagine if the opposite term were constantly applied in writing courses? What would happen?

Key Questions

- What common term or phrased gets used when people talk about your topic?
- How might the opposite or the inverse be true? How might the opposite reveal something interesting?

(5) Advanced Move: Changing the Lens

No matter how hard we try to see things for what they are, we're always seeing the world through a lens. Our comprehension is colored by our culture, upbringing, and our place in history. Consider, for example, how someone born in the late 1800s might respond to a rap music video or the latest television show about zombies. Even some basic reflexes such as amazement or fear are shaped largely by the culture around and within us. Quite often, good writers admit this influence. They acknowledge that their mental reflexes are shaped by their backgrounds and interests. In other words, someone studying psychology learns not only terms and concepts but also ways of understanding data, texts, and situations. A psychologist may look at something such as bullying one way, while a sociologist may see it another.

- Psychologist: Bullying is an expression of personal struggle often created by a difficult home life.
- Sociologist: Bullying is supported by a society that constantly celebrates outward strength, force, and aggression.

These are not simply different definitions but different *ways of seeing*. However, the differences are not set in stone. A sociologist is allowed to think in terms of psychology and vice versa. In other words, people can change their perspectives and change back again. We are not stuck with one lens! With some effort and know-how, we can shift the lenses we've learned (or have been given) and see differently. The result can generate big insights. For example, in an essay titled "Thirteen Ways of Looking at a Crack House," Father Jayme Stayer explores a range of lenses. He begins his essay by explaining his own reaction to first seeing abandoned houses in Detroit, Michigan, places of wreckage and filth. But in the following passage, he describes another perspective, that of a visiting bishop from Africa, who sees the crack houses of Detroit not as a sign of urban blight or abandonment but shelter:

A bishop from Africa was once driven around Detroit and shown the poorest sections of the city. When his host pointed out that the city was eager to tear down the abandoned homes in order to clear away the blight, the African bishop responded that his people would be lucky to live in such houses. From his perspective, those houses weren't miserable hovels or dangerous bonfire-starters. They were shelters from the blazing sun and torrential downpours. Poor Africans who live in shanty towns or refugee camps, the bishop was suggesting, would be happy to have 2000 square feet per family, hard floors to sleep and walk on, and shelter from the heat and rain....

The bishop didn't see the cultural context of those abandoned houses. Unfamiliar with the urban riots, or the cycles of poverty, gang wars and drug violence of the American scene, he didn't know why or how the houses had come to be abandoned. The only thing he saw riding past in his car was shabby, if potentially usable, structures.

Stayer's insight is not simply that abandoned houses can look different to different people. His point is more involved. As he explains below, the different lenses make us ask different questions and come to a better understanding of the subject itself:

Which lens is right cannot be decided until those terms start duking it out inside of an argument: Historically, how did this neighborhood come to be abandoned and why? Politically, what should we now do with the houses? Artistically, how do we portray poverty and for what reasons do we do so?

Activity Prompt: Using Google Earth or MapQuest, you can select different ways to view an area—either with a digital map or from a satellite image. In a small group, access either Google Earth or MapQuest and enter your city or town. Once your area comes up, narrow the focus so that you can see your school or surrounding neighborhood. Then switch the viewer from Map to Satellite. Discuss how the change affects your thinking. How does a satellite image impact your reaction? How is it different from the digital map? And what happens to your thinking if you omit the road and highway labels? How does the world change without them?

Key Questions

- How might someone from a different country or different walk of life see your topic?
- How might someone from a different civilization or point in history see the topic? What problems might they see that you do not?

Writing Prompts

Sometimes, terms simply wear out because a culture moves beyond them. But in academic life, what often happens is this: a scholar senses a problem with a common term and then convinces others of that problem. The change in terminology kicks up the intellectual dust. It makes new ideas possible. As you consider your own project, take one of the following paths:

1. Some of the writers quoted in this chapter reveal the problems with certain terms. They chart out how they've rethought these terms and the specific insights that come from analyzing language. Choose a term in a field of interest that you think deserves closer scrutiny, such as *poetry, art, artistic, patient, file sharing, social networking, piracy*, and so on. In an essay, explain the term as people typically use and understand it. Then, explain the problems with that term. What does the term overlook or miss? How does it misdirect thinking? Then, consider what new term would allow new ideas to grow. Propose this new term to replace the old one and then explain the insights gained from shifting to the proposed term.

2. One way to generate fresh thinking on a topic is to consider the opposite—a term or phrase that represents the *inverse* of established thinking. Choose a term or phrase that you see as limiting or flawed. Then, list some terms or phrases that convey the opposite of the established idea. Select one of these opposites and write an essay that analyzes the new term in light of the old one. What insights emerge from examining the inverse of the original term? Why is this new way of thinking valuable or important for others to consider?

3. Take on a familiar and physical subject (such as a classroom, neighborhood, street, or statue) or a subject from popular culture (such as a film, song, or video). Describe it from your perspective—in the way that you have typically understood it. What has it meant? What is its role or value? And then shift the lens. Try to see the subject with a totally different perspective. For example, how might someone from another culture see the subject? Think of an entirely different person. If you are native-born, try out the perspective of an immigrant. Or if you are liberal, try out the perspective of a conservative. To help you understand the other perspective, apply at least two sources. Bring them in to help explain some quiet assumptions and values associated with the other perspective. As you re-see the subject, what aspects become important? What new tensions come to the surface? What tensions diminish?

8 **Escaping the Status Quo**

Students spend years learning the status quo—all the conventional systems, processes, and boundaries of scholastic life. They learn how to attend classes, when to shift from science to literature, from mathematics to science, from scholastics to sports, and from school to home. Of course, they often ignore the most obvious imperatives. In myriad ways, they resist school's protocols, but even while ignoring what teachers and administrators want, students adopt countless quiet assumptions about right, wrong, real, unreal, and so on. They learn a mountain of beliefs, many unstated, simply by participating in formal education. If teachers are successful and if students are even partly proficient, they adapt to the infrastructure of intellectual life. They take up the usual ways of thinking. In fact, a big part of schooling is just that: learning the conventional modes of thought in all relevant disciplines.

In short, following the rules is key to succeeding in school, work, and domestic life. Most energy spent at school rightly goes to that dimension of human behavior. Teachers lay out formulas, themes, grammar, categories, hierarchies, taxonomies, terms, concepts, and the best practices for operating in public life. However, a significant part of intellectual and writerly success comes from the opposite: strategically abandoning the status quo. Good thinkers in all disciplines (and walks of life) can recognize the limits of commonplace notions and venture beyond them. This doesn't mean they always flout the rules. Nor does it mean they always ignore experts or received wisdom. (The fashionable trend to deny basic truths about the world's shape or the nature of viruses, for instance, comes from other strange forces.) It simply means that successful writing and thinking sometimes depend on a deliberate effort to leave convention behind. And here's something critical: students like it. They enjoy practicing some strategic intellectual mischief. They enjoy the feeling of kicking normality to the curb and heading into some unknown territory. Especially when it's valued and taught as a powerful skill, students are attracted to intellectual mutation.

So when it comes to scholastic and academic life, students learn the intellectual norms, but they should also learn how to manage and sometimes abandon the norms. It's not easy. It requires some powerful moves—but these moves are learnable and highly applicable. This chapter will outline and describe those moves: (1) acknowledging shared assumptions, (2) challenging quiet assumptions, (3) questioning the maxims, (4) questioning the reasoning, (5) breaking up common comparisons.

(1) Acknowledging Shared Assumptions

The first step in escaping the status quo is a simple form of self-awareness. In short, before we escape conventional wisdom, we must admit that we are shaped by it. Even the most distinct individuals are deeply influenced by shared thinking—by a mass of common ideas. It might be easy to imagine that everyone has their own separate thoughts, that we all have our own unique and personalized interior lives, but consider the following passage. It contains various unrelated statements that are shared by most students and teachers:

Other people matter. Tardiness is not a disease. Cows are food; people are not. Fire is not one of my ancestors. Grass does not care to see me. I have an inalienable right to drink water. The past is behind us, the future in front. Falling down can hurt. No matter how hard I flap, I cannot fly without the help of technology. The tooth fairy is a fictional character. Tomorrow, the staircases will lead to the same floors as today. A squirrel will not answer my questions even if I ask nicely. Other people are thinking right now. The moon is real, but it is not an evil force. No one owns Tuesday. Cats are animals rather than plants. Time does not have an opinion, self-esteem problems, or family reunions. The wind is not trying to steal my soul. The sun will rise again.

Those of us who are part of mainstream contemporary life probably accept most or all the preceding statements. And we could list millions more statements like these and thereby prove a certain degree of shared thought. This is not to say that we are all the same—robots or puppets enslaved by a hive mind—but if we are participating in daily life (going to school, going to work, buying products, eating food from grocery store shelves, and so on), we are *automatically* accepting some shared notions about ourselves, other people, and the world around us. These shared notions help to constitute the status quo. They keep things normal.

But the status quo is not simply a list of quiet assumptions. It also involves the way ideas flow along without contest or debate. The statements in the preceding passage, for instance, usually stay below people's radar. They are camouflaged by broad acceptance. This is how the status quo works: it rolls along with quiet agreement. In other words, people generally do not keep redeciding to believe in shared assumptions. Instead, they go about their work, their days, and their leisure time not even wondering about them.

Activity Prompt: Reread the shared assumptions in the previous passage: *Other people matter*, etc. What would happen if we assumed the opposite of many or all of them? Life would quickly get strange. Imagine, for instance, how your nights would change if you believed that the moon was evil. Imagine how you would respond to an evening football game, weather reports, songs, or advertisements about nightlife. Getting along in everyday life would be a challenge. You'd have to duck out of commitments. You'd have to carefully choose dates, jobs, classes, and friends. Now, in a small group, take one of the other statements from the page and imagine how life might look if you all believed the opposite. What practical matters might you have to consider? What other ideas might you accept or dismiss?

Although it's quiet, the status quo shapes our daily lives. All the assumptions we have about the world around us (the wind, the moon, time, Tuesdays, and so on) give shape to the society we inhabit. For instance, we don't have moon protectors in major urban environments. Why? Because most people in our civilization don't see the moon as a threat. And because we don't have moon protectors, most people never think to ask if we should consider them. In other words, widely shared assumptions help to shape the human environment, and that environment, in turn, helps to reinforce widely shared assumptions. It's circular! The usual way of thinking recreates itself over and over again in part because it's easier to live within the established patterns.

The status quo also makes things feel familiar. When we experience something over and over, it becomes normal. And normality is its own kind of camouflage. We get accustomed to seeing something and then learn *not* to see it. For instance, imagine a world without electrical wires running along highways. Imagine that all of the telephone poles and cables that currently line much of the country are gone. And then imagine someone coming along and suggesting that we should cut down millions of trees, strip off the branches, and post them along most of the roads for the purpose of carrying electricity to towns and cities. Imagine how people would respond to such an incredible suggestion. It'd be unthinkable. But because we're accustomed to seeing all the poles and wires, they are, in a way, invisible. This is how normal creates a way of seeing and not seeing.

Activity Prompt: Consider the *infrastructure* of your community: the buildings, roads, traffic lights, drainage ditches, gutters, electrical grid, fences, and so on. All of those structural features are designed to keep daily life working. Without a sound infrastructure, people would find it difficult, or impossible, to carry out a schedule—to have regular meetings, get products to stores, ship crops, buy food, meet with clients, talk with students, answer emails, or post blogs. The infrastructure maintains a status quo, or usual state of affairs. In a small group, discuss the ways you each reinforce the usual state of affairs. What behaviors and statements align with and support the normal way of doing things? Why do you go along? What forces keep you in line?

(2) Challenging Quiet Assumptions

Despite the power of normality, people sometimes come along and challenge a quietly shared assumption. People in our daily lives sometimes push against the normal intellectual flow, and they do this because the normal way of doing things has become stale, inefficient, bogged down, or just plain bad. For instance, consider the shift in school classrooms: several decades ago, nearly all classrooms were structured to support lectures. All desks or seats faced forward. Now, classrooms are often structured to support group work, discussion, and interaction. At some point, enough people understood the need for drastic change.

Sometimes, the status quo conceals an ongoing mistake—an error in judgment or practice that comes to light only after someone recognizes it as such. In fact, academic and professional work often attempts to do just that: to recognize the intellectual and practical errors that people keep missing. Scholars in all academic disciplines try, as best they can, to understand the power of the status quo—to realize when the usual way of doing things becomes a problem or hindrance. And that person, whoever introduces change, might at first seem strange or awkward to everyone else.

Good thinkers and writers learn to question some aspects of the status quo. They root out assumptions, put them under the intellectual microscope, and evaluate their worth. For example, the following passage roots out a basic assumption about government and democracy:

> *Politicians and media personalities are making the case that democracy in the US is under attack. Politicians from both parties have argued that we could lose our democracy. And when they say this, they often describe the biggest threats: corporate money, splinter groups within the military, or self-serving political figures. The threat, then, is often portrayed as a powerful person or institution. But average citizens can also be undemocratic. We the people threaten the very processes we value. Voters across political parties treat our favorite politicians like celebrities. We want them to be loved, to be hailed, even adored. We want them to have ultimate power against their opponents. We want them to win at any cost, assuming they will always make the right decisions. It's a naïve and dangerous form of support.*

Of course, not all quiet assumptions harm people and society. Some simply keep things running along. They maintain the infrastructure so we can communicate and carry on with public life. But when quiet and "normal" assumptions work against people, when they limit how we think, good writers and thinkers call them out.

Judging the status quo comes easy when we look to the past. With the clarity of hindsight, we can look at any decade, year, or month and judge what was deemed normal thinking. For example, people who grew up in the nineteenth and twentieth centuries operated with some basic assumptions that have since been dismissed:

- Women are naturally less scientific than men.
- Men are more competitive than women.
- There are two types of thinkers: right-brained and left-brained.
- Children are better at learning than adults.

For decades, even centuries, such notions held sway. They operated quietly in countless arguments, policies, and formal statements. However, due to discoveries in biology and neurology, most people no longer believe such notions. The status quo changed. And if we go centuries further back, we can see some notions that we, today, consider wildly incorrect:

- Witches can make people sick.
- The sun revolves around the Earth.
- Sickness can be cured by making patients bleed.

From our current position in the twenty-first century, much of the past seems painfully ignorant. But we should be cautious about the present as well. We should not assume that new or current thinking is automatically more correct than past thinking. Let's not forget that engineers still cannot fathom how the Great Pyramids were built or how Roman aqueducts were conceived. In fact, plenty of scholars find that ancient viewpoints offer more insight than anything in recent times. In short, the passage of time does not always generate better thinking. Despite our technological prowess (cell phones that arrange our days and GPS units that tell us where to turn), humans may be increasingly more confused about plenty. Good thinkers have to consider the past and the present with healthy doubt.

Key Question

What quiet and widely shared assumption might be incorrect?

(3) Questioning the Maxims

Maxims are repeated, familiar statements. They are uttered in all walks of life, and their repetition makes them *seem* true. Consider some of the maxims that creep into all forms of public discussion and debate:

Opposites attract.

Actions speak louder than words.

No pain, no gain.

Whatever doesn't kill you only makes you stronger.

A picture is worth a thousand words.

Beauty is only skin deep.

Beggars can't be choosers.

Blood is thicker than water.

Experience is the best teacher.

The bigger they are, the harder they fall.

The eyes are the window to the soul.

Time is money.

Honesty is the best policy.

Such statements rarely get challenged. In fact, they often settle discussions, stop thinking, and make everyone involved nod in agreement. But they can be entirely wrong. For instance, experience might be a costly and inefficient teacher, a thousand words might be far more valuable than one picture, opposites might repel one another, and plenty of things that don't kill you might drain your spirit or sap your energy.

Any given topic likely comes along with maxims. Whether it's politics ("You can't trust government"), work ("Another day, another dollar"), domestic life ("Home is where the heart is"), or even kids ("Boys will be boys"), any topic seems to attract a certain number of familiar sentiments that keep the same old thinking in place. But good writers sometimes go after the maxims. They call them out and challenge the thinking. For example, the following passage takes on a common statement about strength:

> So many ads now rely on personal strength to sell products. Migraine medication, adult diapers, home insurance, bank loans, cell phones, and plenty more products get sold with some slogan or claim about an individual's personal strength. It may all come down to the old assertion: **only the strong survive**. Of course, it's pleasing to imagine oneself as strong, that survival depends upon one's own force and power, but the old assertion is simply not true. Survival does not depend on strength but on a host of other factors, most of them beyond an individual's control. In fact, survival in a complex society means relying on others' products and services—on a network of tools, medications, transportation systems, satellites, sewers, and communications. People lead longer and better lives because they have easy access to good food, clean water, and sanitary conditions, not because they're able to lift weight, swing a weapon, or stand firm against enemies.
>
> America's thoughtless love affair with strength—as the ultimate personal quality—hides some difficult truths. For instance, prisons are full of strong people, those with both physical force and mental determination. The wrong decisions, not lack of strength, put them behind bars. As it turns out, the ability to see long-term consequences and act accordingly far outweighs personal strength. While being clear-headed and thoughtful doesn't sell many products, such intellectual qualities have better track records for surviving in a complex world.

The writer here interrogates the soundness of a widely accepted statement—along with its value system. This is the power of questioning maxims: the process ultimately brings writers face-to-face with widely shared truths or widely shared illusions. The process, however, takes some time. Because the maxims are so familiar, so normal sounding, they must be sniffed out and carefully dismissed.

Activity Prompt: Education is full of maxims—claims that show up repeatedly and without debate or discussion. Consider one of the following statements. Explain why it might, despite its ring of truth, be questionable:

Everyone learns differently.

You have to learn the rules before you can break them.

You have to believe in yourself.

When the student is ready, the teacher appears.

Key Questions

Consider a topic or issue you are writing about and ask the following:

- What maxims are related to that topic? What do people typically say about the topic, the debate, and the behaviors associated with it?
- How might the maxim miss something? How might it be inaccurate?

(4) Questioning Common Reasons

The status quo relies on a system of reasons (like those explained in Chapter 4). Often, those reasons sit quietly. But if the status quo is to be questioned, its reasoning must be brought into the light of day. It's no easy task, but the rewards are high. When writers carefully examine common, everyday reasoning, they can create powerful insights. For example, the following passage examines the reasoning behind a common statement about learning:

> *It's often said that people learn differently. But this belief comes primarily from different abilities or different academic strengths. If a student is successful at mathematics, they are assumed to think in some mathematical fashion and therefore learn all subject matter in that same fashion. People might even say they are mathematical learners—that they have mathematical brains. But those are giant logical leaps. Students who are good at mathematics don't necessarily learn differently from a student who's done well in language arts. Success in a subject comes from a range of social and personal issues, not necessarily a permanent mental operation. It's an error to imagine that differences in performance automatically come from different types of brains.*

This passage points to a logical problem or *fallacy* known as non sequitur (described below). While there are many such logical problems—with a range of names—the following three tend to haunt common wisdom:

> *The Wrong Cause: Sometimes called faulty cause/effect, this problem involves seeing a causal relation where one may not exist. In recent years, for instance, thousands of parents in the United States have blamed vaccinations for autism. They cite a range of studies that show a correlation between vaccinations and the first signs of autistic behavior. But they may be confusing correlation with causation since autistic behavior often becomes apparent at roughly the same time children get immunization shots. The scientists who have fought this faulty cause/effect reasoning have argued that autism may, in fact, have many causes (both genetic and environmental) and may lie deep in early embryonic brain development.*

> *The Wrong Name: This may also be called the wrong category. The problem here is one of definition. When we give something a name, we define it and then act according to that definition. Names create a way of thinking. For example, during the past several decades, the US government has been waging a **war on***

drugs. In some ways, the phrase seems to fit the situation: soldiers are sometimes involved, arms are traded and sold, people get killed. But as many sociologists, and a few politicians, have pointed out, **war on drugs** is simply the wrong phrase because the soldier/enemy metaphor ignores how drug addiction is an internal enemy, requiring counseling rather than hand grenades and tanks.

The Wrong Conclusion: We often leap to conclusions. Something happens, then something else happens, and we generate a finalizing statement: "Even though I tried, I failed my first English course, so I'm just not good at writing." The logical problem here is that the conclusion doesn't necessarily follow from what is known. A huge range of conditions may have resulted in someone failing an English course. But those conditions do not figure into the conclusion "I'm not good at writing." The problem lies not in the truth or falsehood of the conclusion but in the way a conclusion gets developed: too many logical steps get skipped. Sometimes called a **non sequitur**, this logical problem haunts our daily lives, and it lurks in formal written work as well.

The bigger problem with all these logical flaws is that they can result in ideas that get widely accepted and then established in the status quo. Once something becomes finalized, published, and widely accepted, it's often hard to question. But calling out the flawed logic can change everything. Simply calling attention to the logical problem in a common phrase or stated conclusion can disrupt the status quo. Like pulling a single brick from the bottom of a tower, good thinkers sometimes bring down a whole intellectual contraption that would otherwise have stood with its flaws.

Key Question

Consider flaws or *fallacies* in a common way of thinking (about your chosen topic or issue). Might people often assume the wrong cause, use the wrong name, or come to the wrong conclusion?

(5) Advanced Move: Breaking Up Common Comparisons

Sometimes common wisdom comes packaged in a nice comparison. But comparisons, like terms and reasons, can be challenged. When writers challenge a comparison, they break apart two ideas or concepts that have been joined. In other words, they find something wrong with the marriage of two ideas. The following passage attempts to break up a recent and widely expressed comparison:

> Ads often call dog owners **pet parents** or **dog parents**. Such phrases rely on a basic comparison between children and pets. Having children, the thinking goes, is like having pets. There are some similarities, no doubt. Dog owners, like parents of children, may love their pets. They may worry about them, care for them in countless ways, devoting money and time to their wellbeing, but there's a crucial difference between parenting children and owning a dog: parents **raise** a child. They develop their children's capacity to leave home, enter the society, and build their own lives. In other words, they develop citizens that must go on and contribute to the world. Pet owners may **train** their animals, but they don't raise them. That crucial difference gets brushed over whenever someone says **pet parents**.

The writer could keep going and explain how raising a child impacts parents' daily decisions and how those decisions differ from those of pet owners. As the writing continues, it would likely reveal some interesting emotional and practical differences between the two groups.

For another example, consider the widely accepted comparison between a human brain and a computer. Teachers, parents, and even doctors rely on the comparison to understand how learning works. But the comparison may create a misunderstanding of brain function. The writer of the next passage gets personal but still makes the key move in breaking apart the comparison:

> I constantly hear language that compares people to computers. For instance, a journalist recently said we are "hardwired" for some basic activities. And recently, my uncle explained how he needed a new memory card because he couldn't recall a date. The list goes on. It's become normal to see human thinking and computer thinking in the same light. But people are not computers primarily because we are built for change. Learning actually means changing how our brains respond to the world—to a problem, a story, an equation, a painting, any stimulus at all. As AI becomes widely used and more developed, computers will, like humans, learn to morph their own processing powers. For now, it's still a bad comparison because whenever we insist that humans are hardwired, we forget the essence of human learning.

When writers take on the status quo and nudge something out of place, they may leave a hole in common thinking. In many respects, they leave a hole in reality! The comfortable conclusions, the nicely smoothed-over walls of normality, are suddenly gone. Not always, but often, writers try to fill the hole they've created. They turn away from the comfortable and consider something different—a new idea, a new conclusion, a new comparison. This is hard work because new ideas, generally speaking, do not fit as well as old ones, which have had time to settle in and become normal. Foreign ideas are harder to process, harder to digest. But good writers work to make the foreign ideas acceptable.

Activity Prompt: Consider another common comparison. In a small group, list the ways the two ideas or concepts are different. What factors show up in one and not the other?

Key Question

Consider your chosen topic—whatever issue you're arguing about or researching. Make a list of all the comparisons that are made when people write or speak about the topic. How might one of those comparisons miss something? How might one of those comparisons get something wrong?

Writing Prompts

Much academic work may seem strange or out of touch with common sense. By design, many scholarly projects set out to move thinking away from the limitations or inaccuracies of established thought. Consider one of the following paths for developing your own project that escapes the status quo:

1. Examine a common practice in education, one that is widely and quietly accepted. Consider some practice that is so widely accepted that your peers and teachers *wouldn't even think* to question it. Apply the moves in this chapter: Call out quiet assumptions related to the practice—for instance, assumptions about learning, success, or knowledge. Question maxims and the logic that keeps the practice in place. Break up any comparisons that come along with the practice.

2. Examine a popular form of entertainment such as basketball or NASCAR. Write an essay that explains how that form of entertainment reinforces the status quo. How does it support common ways of thinking about people, success, men, women, and individuality? Even if it appears, to most people, like a break in the routine—like something that pushes against the mainstream—consider how it might *actually* uphold widely accepted modes of living. Consider the common images, celebrities, and behaviors associated with the form of entertainment. How do they reinforce the status quo?

3. How are you stuck in the status quo? Write a reflective essay that describes your own participation in the normal modes of living. What quiet assumptions about your community, your neighbors, or your schools do you accept? What keeps you believing? What keeps you from rejecting the norm? What hopes or fears are built into your acceptance of the status quo? What lessons, messages, or maxims maintain those hopes or fears?

9 **Reflecting**

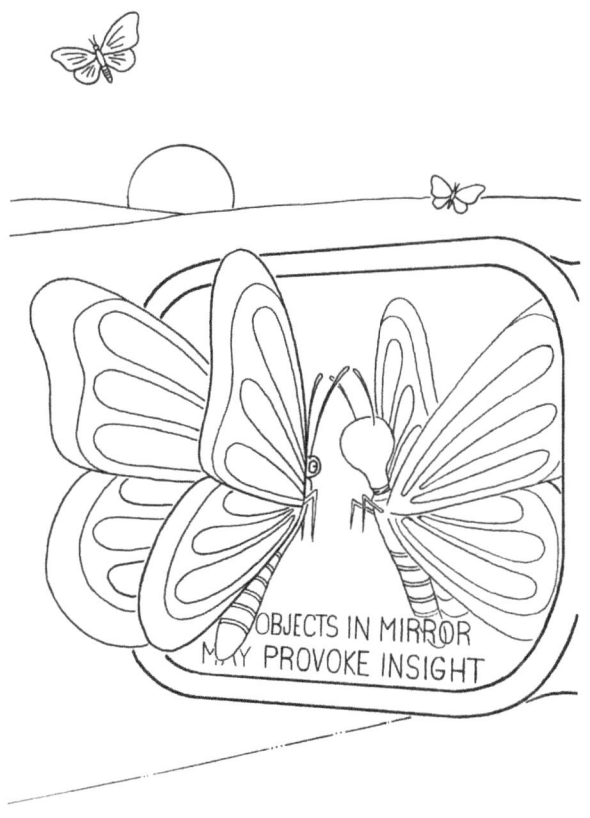

Self-assessment has been widely adopted in writing pedagogy. Its value is well-established and highly regarded. In fact, it's so important that many high school and college writing courses now contain formal assignments (portfolios, self-critique essays) that invite students to assess their own progress over an academic term. However, as with any well-established assignment type, students may sometimes not appreciate the function of self-assessment. Put another way, we teachers may sometimes not fully celebrate the pure power of self-assessment. For this reason, it's crucial to remind students that professionals in all fields devote countless hours to examining and judging their own performance: football coaches record games and inspect each play, dancers practice in front of mirrors, engineers inspect their methods at every step, actors study their gestures on camera, and comedians record their acts and carefully analyze their timing. Whether we're talking about writers, artists, musicians, engineers, or athletes, people get better at their crafts when they self-assess. To improve, they must do more than practice. They must examine past behavior, analyze what did or didn't work, and then readjust.

Writers of all kinds must learn to see their own ideas from a distance. It's difficult but necessary. When writers genuinely revise their work, they discover gaps, grammatical fumbles, stylistic issues, logical problems, and underdeveloped ideas. But most importantly, with enough guidance, they can also discover possibilities. With the right questions and impulses in place, writers can return to their own work and find untapped ideas, new claims, and nuances lurking in between their own sentences. In this sense, genuine revision can be a final, sometimes explosive, bout of invention.

For these reasons, reflection assignments are increasingly important. These assignments give students a chance to record their thoughts and judge their own progress, to explain, in their own words, how they understand course goals and the extent to which they've achieved them. In a reflection essay or letter, students refer to specific intellectual tasks they performed. They seek complexity and tension in their own past selves. They call out and examine past assumptions. They try to understand their own quiet operations.

Reflective assignments often have stated criteria—or standards of judgment for examining performance. Here are some sample criteria for a reflective assignment:

- The main idea of the reflection is appropriately focused and readily accessible to the reader.
- The main idea is sufficiently supported and well-developed throughout the reflection.
- The reflection thoroughly explains how your ideas evolved or changed over the course of the assignment.
- The reflection clearly shows how you developed a new insight.

In such criteria, words like "appropriately," "readily," "sufficiently," "thoroughly," and "clearly" point to the evaluation taking place. Student work is assessed based on how well it meets each of the established criteria. An essay might achieve one goal, another moderately well, and another not so well. But despite the individual criteria, the goal of these assignments usually involves intensive and detailed examination of the student's own thinking. The most successful writing, then, provides thorough and focused explanations of changes, stumbles, small steps, and leaps forward in one's own thinking.

But self-assessment, and reflection more broadly, need not come at the end of a writing project or academic term. These mental operations can be strategic writerly moves throughout the process. They can also be major elements of informative and argumentative essays, even formal reports. The point here is that reflection is widely hailed as a valuable educational tool, but the act should also be seen as another intellectual move in a writer's toolbox. This brief chapter offers two key moves for reflection: 1) examining past assumptions and 2) describing new thinking. They can be integrated into countless writing projects.

(1) Examining Past Assumptions

Lived experiences can sometimes crash against our thinking and force us to change a position. And sometimes the force is enough to make us reconsider our own thoughts—our own assumptions about what is good, bad, real, or unreal. In these moments, we are thrown into a kind of intensive self-assessment. We ask ourselves not only what we think but also *what we didn't even know we thought*. Examining past assumptions often means evaluating old prejudices that were passed along to us, biases that somehow became routine thoughts. In the following passage, taken from an argumentative essay about musical training, a writer describes his own past assumptions:

> Years ago, I assumed that my singing voice was natural. In other words, I believed that my automatic way of singing was the most natural, therefore genuine. But when I began formal training in choir and in private lessons, I realized I'd been singing wrong. At first, I was resistant to the idea—to the basic notion that I could use my own voice incorrectly. It was my voice after all! But I learned that young singers often sing with the very same reflexes (and muscles) they use for casual conversation. They simply make their words longer and louder. The problem is that we don't typically talk with diaphragm support. We push sound through our throats and form words with our teeth, lips, and tongue. But singing, the kind of singing that makes careers, requires a

different posture, a different set of muscles. And only after much practice does a singer learn the difference between conversational voice and singing voice. It's not just a matter of extending one's words!

My experience reveals a false belief that many young artists and athletes carry around. Our initial reflexes aren't necessarily the most beneficial, even the most natural. We can come at a practice, art, or skill in the exact wrong way and, therefore, make our bodies work in unnatural ways. We can injure our voices, arms, backs, and joints. For example, my friend Aaron is in baseball. After two seasons, he developed elbow pain. As a pitcher, his injury threatened his role on the team and even his future in the sport. After months of retraining, he learned to throw the ball differently. His new approach may save his arm and his future.

*Anyone entering an artform or sport must get beyond a flawed belief in their most automatic reflexes. They must be open to relearning what their bodies do and **can** do. At a basic level, artists and athletes aren't simply training to learn a craft; they're training their own impulses. And that training can get short-circuited if they hold onto unhelpful beliefs.*

This writer uses personal experience to make a broader point about artistic and athletic training. The knowledge he builds through training allows him to realize his misconceptions, the false beliefs that had crept into his thinking over time. In this way, self-assessment can be more than discovery. It can become a powerful source of argumentation.

Activity Prompts:

1. As a class or group, reflect on your assumptions about writing: its relationship to thinking, its role in education, and its connection to the world beyond school. List the assumptions that come to mind. Which assumptions are beneficial? Which need to be rethought?

2. In a discussion group, recall your early educational experiences. Make a list of criteria that teachers used to assess your performance. Even if they weren't stated directly (as they often are in assignment prompts), how did you know about them? How did you know what to strive for, what to avoid, or what to fix? How did you know about the difference between excellent work and satisfactory work—or between passing and failing?

(2) Describing New Thinking

Good writers are usually good at describing their own thinking. In other words, they're good at detailing the intellectual changes they experience. They try, as best they can, to sense moments of separation from a past belief to a new one. For example, in the following excerpt from a reflective essay, a literature student explains a flaw in her past approach and a different way of going forward:

> *In preparing to write an analysis of* **Othello,** *I was lost on where to begin. The greatest breakthrough for me was when I reflected on my earlier self assessments and feedback. I realized I should first choose passages and analyze them, gradually moving to the creation of a thesis, as opposed to creating a thesis and searching desperately for evidence to support it. Before I do anything, I should let a work reveal itself to me.*

In the past, this writer began assignments with a thesis statement and then hunted for passages to prove that thesis. But after reflecting on the approach and considering feedback from teachers, she realized a more fruitful strategy: letting ideas gradually develop into a thesis. In this case, the writer stepped outside of her own practice, saw herself from a distance, and, as a result, shifted her approach.

Sometimes, reflecting on one's own practices leads to self-assessment and a dramatic shift. Writers change their minds, literally, and disavow a previous perspective or behavior. In the following passage, a writer admits a major change in his thinking. In fact, he describes a "misconception" that guided his behavior for years:

> *Through junior and high school, I associated a busy schedule with success. If my days were full of classes, practice, and homework, I thought I was being productive. I joined soccer, concert band, marching band, Spanish Club, and drama. But it was all too much. As classes became more difficult, I couldn't manage everything well. Only recently did I realize my own misconception, my erroneous belief that running from one appointment to another said something good about me. Now I realize the opposite: running from one thing to another was a sign that I'd over-committed. But more importantly, my schedule kept me from focusing on any specific course or activity. Without focus, I fell behind in nearly everything.*

> There are only so many hours, and each cannot be filled with tasks. Doing many different things in a day is not a sign of productivity. Instead, it's an invitation to scattered thoughts. As tasks become more involved, more sophisticated, they demand longer periods of attention, more hours of reading, studying, practicing. At some point, I needed to realize that. I was bound for a life of mediocre grades and frustrated efforts outside of school. Given some direct guidance from a teacher, I have turned my thinking and my daily regime around. I gave up on drama and Spanish Club. I stuck with band because it's been a source of friendship, support, and learning. And beyond the formal school day, I now insist on at least two hours alone each evening. In those hours, I settle into my work. I no longer squeeze in a range of obligations. Instead, I push away anything competing for my attention. With intensive focus and plenty of unscripted hours, I'm experiencing new levels of success.

Here, the writer describes an important development. He once attempted to load his schedule. Now he works to unload it. And what's important in these passages is that he doesn't merely explain the difference in his actions (*I did that and now I do this*). Instead, he describes the thinking responsible for that difference.

Assessing our thinking doesn't always produce major "aha" moments. Sometimes, our insights are more subtle, less defined. We've come around to some new way of thinking, but we haven't yet reached any firm conclusions or clear solutions. And that's okay. In fact, explaining *where we are now* is often powerful.

Activity Prompts

1. In a small group, discuss experiences you've had with writer's block. What did you do to overcome it? What specific strategies did you use to start writing? Which of these strategies could you pull forward to a current situation you're experiencing?

2. Consider common knee-jerk reactions like road rage or impatience at the checkout line. As a group, talk about experiences you've had in which you've snapped out of some patterned way of thinking. What prompted you to rethink the situation, your behavior, or your own thinking?

Key Questions

An assumption is a basic belief that operates quietly in our thinking. It rarely gets voiced or questioned. But identifying and revising our assumptions generates good thinking and sometimes powerful passages. Consider a topic you're writing about and then make a list of all your basic beliefs related to that topic. For each basic belief, ask yourself if the opposite could be true, partly true, or equally true. In other words, might the opposite belief have *some* truth to it? If so, how does that impact your thinking? How does it impact what you've said or written? How might it change your behavior? What new insights emerge?

Writing Prompts

Rethinking our thinking sounds like hard work. And it is. But with clear intellectual maneuvers, reflection and self-assessment can become routine, a reflex that helps us in *all* our intellectual pursuits. Consider one of the following paths:

1. If you're like most people, you judge yourself. You judge your behavior in social settings, your skill level in academics or sports, maybe even your reflex to be kind or cruel. But all forms of judging depend on some criteria—on certain standards of behavior beyond the specific situation. In an essay, explain what criteria you use to assess your own behavior. Where did those criteria come from? Did someone teach them to you? Did you pick them up from watching someone else? What, if anything, would you change about the way you assess yourself?

2. Think about something you understand well, like a particular academic subject or a personal interest. Reflect on your knowledge. How did you come to understand it? What specific behaviors or ways of thinking did you adopt to hone your expertise? Consider if you denied any past assumptions in order to become better at this task. As your understanding developed, did you find yourself having to change your perspective or dismiss old beliefs? What happened? Consider how you know you're good at this activity in the first place. What criteria do you apply to measure your success? Did you develop your own criteria, or were they established for you?

Describe the process of becoming an expert to readers who might not be familiar with your interests.

3. Consider an error in thinking you've made in the past—not a simple mistake but a bad judgment or flawed position. Maybe you misjudged someone or refused to acknowledge something about a situation. Maybe you overestimated your own abilities or didn't fully appreciate your own naivety. Concentrate not only on your actions but also on the assumptions behind them. Also consider the ways you talked yourself into believing yourself. What reasoning did you use? What did you actively ignore? Write an essay that explains the intellectual operations behind your flawed thinking. (You might also try to explain how you came through to some better, richer way of thinking.)

10 Mapping the Moves

The following pages offer outlines for structuring different essay projects. There are many options. Which one is best? It depends on the assignment, purpose, and topic. The outlines presented here provide general steps that can be drawn out, minimized, or even skipped depending on the project. The idea here is that the moves explained in previous chapters can be used in combinations that accommodate a range of writing projects. The outlines are not meant to be restrictive or confining but to provide a path, a way forward for students who need (and benefit from) a general map. Of course, once they begin writing, students might turn back, redirect, and reshape. But having an initial pattern will help to guide their energy—to aim their thinking and not struggle for hours (or days or weeks) to imagine the next step. As you will see, this chapter groups outlines under typical assignment types:

- Explanatory or Descriptive
- Analytical
- Argumentative
- Reflective

Explanatory or Descriptive Projects

The purpose of these projects is to understand something better—to bring a topic, person, or field of study into better focus. The goal is not to argue against or for a position but to look closely, to develop a keen awareness, and even to generate meaning about something, someone, or someplace. Such assignments may be ethnographies, histories, or profiles. They will primarily use the moves described in Chapter 1, "Seeking Complexity"; Chapter 2, "Applying a Concept"; Chapter 5, "Applying Sources"; and Chapter 6, "Seeking Tension."

Some explanatory/descriptive assignments ask that writers examine an ongoing debate or contested issue—that they come to understand the subject well enough to offer clarity and insight. Such assignments are not argumentative: they don't invite writers to take a stand but, instead, to explain the nature of the positions. Here is one common approach: The writers start with a real situation or event, give readers enough information to understand what happened, and explain any tension at play. Here, they might bring in a source to further explain the situation. Next, they describe the tension in detail. Who is debating? What bigger issue is the debate about? Other sources may help to describe the debate or add dimension to the different sides. They may make connections to other situations, events, or issues. Finally, they come back to the original situation or event and explain how it can be seen differently or more fully:

Describe a real situation related to the subject.

- Give details about the event.
- Explain the tension at play.

Draw from a vital source.

- Describe how it characterizes the situation.
- Describe how it characterizes the tension.

Describe the tension.

- Use specific terms to describe a debate related to the subject.
- Integrate a source that describes the tension.
- Make a connection to a broader tension.
- Explain how you see the situation differently or more fully.
- Explain why it matters to those involved.
- Explain what new questions or problems emerge.

Writers might also start with a broad tension (Chapter 6). They bring in a representative source that characterizes the debate. Then, they describe a specific situation from personal experience or from research that relates to the broad tension. They may also make connections between the situation and another that readers might identify with. Finally, they come back to the broad tension and explain how it can be seen differently or more fully:

Describe a broad tension.

- Use specific terms to describe the debate.
- Integrate a source that describes the tension.

Show the tension in a real situation.

- Give details about the situation.
- Integrate a source that helps to characterize the situation.

Make connections to other situations.

- Explain an idea or point you can draw from the comparison.
- Explain how the situation resembles a dissimilar situation.

Explain how you understand the tension differently or more fully.

- Explain why it matters to those involved.
- Explain what new questions or problems emerge.

Some assignments in this category ask students to examine (even define) an idea or concept. Such projects often start with a source as a doorway. Writers begin by explaining how the source uses the term or concept in question. If the concept is particularly complex, writers might compare it to something common or familiar. Then, they describe a common association or two—what ideas usually come along with the concept. Writers can then make an advanced move by denying those usual associations or explaining how they misdirect or hinder people's thinking. Next, writers carefully unpack the concept. They show the qualities that people might overlook, the traits or parts that are often ignored. Finally, writers might get personal and explain how this process has changed their own thinking:

Explain the term or concept.

- Refer to a source that uses the term or concept.
- Explain how it is used.
- Compare it to something familiar.

Deny a usual association.

- Explain how the association is misleading.
- Explain how the association is limited.

Unpack the term or concept.

- Describe qualities that might be taken for granted.
- Describe effects that aren't immediately apparent.

Explain how you see things differently.

- Explain how you understand the concept more fully.
- Describe questions or uncertainties you still have.

Writers can also start this project type without a source. First, they describe ways people normally use a term or concept. They might also compare it to something familiar to help readers understand how it functions. Then, they start unpacking. They take the term or concept apart and try to discover three, four, or more major components. They often use separate paragraphs to thoroughly explain what others might overlook. They can also describe any dualities at work. They may take a paragraph to explain the middle ground, the gray area between the two extremes. Finally, they come back around to the term or concept and explain any new insights that come from this close inspection:

Explain a term or concept.

- Explain how the term or concept is used.
- Compare the term or concept to something familiar.

Unpack the term or concept.

- Describe qualities that might be taken for granted.
- Describe effects that aren't immediately apparent.

Bust up a duality.

- Describe the duality: On the one side, there's: _____ and on the other, there's: _____
- Explain how the duality is misleading or limited.
- Describe the gray area: between the two extremes, there's another possibility.

Explain how you see things differently.

- Explain how you understand the term or concept more fully.
- Describe questions or uncertainties you still have.

Analytical Projects

These projects aim to break something down, to take apart or dismantle a specific subject such as a photograph, an advertisement, a written argument, a piece of literature, or even a concept or theory. The goal is not to judge or celebrate the subject but simply to take it seriously, to examine it so closely that writers (and readers) come to a better understanding. Such projects will rely on Chapter 1, "Seeking Complexity"; Chapter 2, "Applying Concepts"; Chapter 3, "Analyzing Arguments"; Chapter 5, "Applying Sources"; and Chapter 6, "Seeking Tension."

Some analytical assignments ask writers to dissect complex concepts. In such cases, writers often start by explaining the concept in detail, giving readers background information to understand the various layers. Then they compare the concept to something that is common or familiar to readers. They may also explain how the concept normally gets used or applied. They may ask what the concept helps people to do or understand. Here, they may apply supportive sources. Then, they apply the concept to a particular situation, text, or case. Finally, they show what that application reveals:

Explain a concept related to the subject.

- Use specific language to describe the concept.
- Compare it to something familiar.

Explain how the concept gets used.

- Give an example of the concept being applied.
- Integrate a source that uses the concept.

Apply the concept to a real situation.

- Explain what problems the application solves.
- Explain what insights emerge.
- Explain what new questions or problems emerge.

Explain how you see things differently.

- Explain how you understand the concept more fully.
- Describe questions or uncertainties you still have.

Some projects ask writers to look outside their field of study to analyze a concept. The writers begin by examining the concept, describing it in detail. For especially complex concepts, they make connections to other familiar ideas. They may explain where the concept comes from and how it shows up in daily life, writing, and speaking. For this step, they integrate a source that uses the concept. Then, they transport the concept into another discipline. Finally, they explain how the concept creates a better way of thinking, a more accurate vision, or a more thorough understanding:

Explain a concept related to the subject.

- Use specific language to describe the concept.
- Compare it to something familiar.

Explain how the concept gets used.

- Give an example of the concept being applied.
- Integrate a source that uses the concept.

Transport the concept into another discipline.

- Explain what problems the concept solves.
- Explain what insights emerge.
- Explain what new questions or problems emerge.

Explain how you see things differently.

- Explain how you understand the concept more fully.
- Describe questions or uncertainties you still have

Often, analytical projects ask writers to break down elements within a written argumentative text—an essay, blog, or article. For such analyses, writers often begin by explaining the issue or topic within the target text. If the text deals with a broad tension, they describe that tension for readers, applying sources if necessary. Then, they examine the context surrounding the work. Finally, they analyze the reasoning of the work. They may also consider specific words or arrangement strategies of the target text:

Summarize ideas within the target text.

- Examine the issue and how the text characterizes it.
- Explain the text's key insight or main claim.
- Describe the writer's purpose

Consider the context surrounding the text.

- Describe the cultural atmosphere.
- Describe the political climate.

Analyze the reasoning of the text.

- Describe the claim of the text.
- Explain all the reasons supporting the main claim.
- Explain how evidence supports the reasons.
- Explain how the claim relates to the tension surrounding the text.

Explain new insights about the text.

- Explain how the claim, reasoning, or evidence sheds light on the issue itself.
- Or explain how the claim, reasoning, or evidence relates to something in the context.

Or instead of focusing on a written text, writers might analyze the elements of a nontextual work, such as a work of art or architecture. In this case, they can start by investigating the purpose of the work. They make connections between the work and another work, event, or situation that readers might identify with. Then, they examine the physical and cultural context of the work. Finally, they examine the quiet argument that the work is making and explain what artistic elements contribute to the main (perhaps unstated) claim:

Examine the purpose of a work.

- Explain the original intention for the work.
- Explain how the purpose has changed over time.

Find patterns in other works.

- Explain how the work resembles something similar.
- Explain how the work resembles something dissimilar.
- Explain an idea you can draw from the comparison.

Consider the context surrounding the work.

- Describe the physical setting.
- Describe the cultural atmosphere.
- Describe the political climate.

Analyze the quiet argument of the work.

- Describe the message of the work.
- Explain how the message relates to the work's purpose.
- Explain how the message relates to the context surrounding the work.

Argumentative Projects

The purpose of these projects is to make a case for a stated position. Often, the goal is to persuade others to see a subject in a certain way or to propose a particular course of action. These assignments ask writers first to think critically about a topic, and then to argue for a position related to that topic. Such assignments include proposals, argumentative research essays, and literary arguments. They rely mainly on moves described in Chapter 1, "Seeking Complexity"; Chapter 4, "Justifying a Position"; Chapter 5, "Applying Sources"; Chapter 6, "Seeking Tension"; Chapter 7, "Inspecting the Terms"; and Chapter 8, "Escaping the Status Quo."

Argumentative assignments often require writers to assert a claim and to justify that claim with reasoning and evidence. Writers begin by describing the context or situation—in other words, why an argument is necessary or ongoing in the first place. This means they are describing the tension—specific and/or broad. Then, they offer their position on the matter. They go on to give reasoning and supportive evidence, bringing in supportive sources to back up their points. The most successful writers slowly walk readers through reasoning, devoting entire paragraphs to complex chunks of information. They may also consider both the subtle tensions and the broad tensions at play—conceding or qualifying points where appropriate. They may help readers understand tension by making connections to other situations, events, or issues they may be familiar with. Finally, they come back to their original claim and explain how this process has expanded their thinking:

Explain the situation.

- Describe the issue or tension that needs to be addressed.
- Offer your position, your specific claim.

Line up reasoning and evidence to support the claim.

- Give each reason individually.
- Explain any evidence that supports each one.
- Integrate a source that describes the evidence.

Deny the opposition.

- Identify an opposing position.
- Analyze the opposition's reasoning.
- Concession: describe any value within the opposition's reasoning.
- Counterargument: explain how the opposition is limited or flawed.

Explain the value of your position.

- Explain how your position matters, what it offers.
- Or explain how your position offers new insights or helpful questions.

Some writers highlight their reasoning more than all other elements. They may still begin by explaining the surrounding context and then their particular claim. Then, they slowly break down their reasons. If the reasons are especially complex, they devote entire paragraphs to each. They may integrate sources to help back up points. They may explain how their reasons connect to a broad principle related to the topic, asking why people should care or how that principle may affect them. Finally, they come back to their original claim and explain how it adds value.

Explain the situation

- Describe the issue or tension that needs to be addressed.
- Offer your position, your specific claim.

Break down the reasons for the claim.

- Explain each reason.
- Integrate a source that supports the reason.
- Connect to a broad principle.

Deny the opposition.

- Identify an opposing position.
- Analyze the opposition's reasoning.
- Concession: describe any value within the opposition's reasoning.
- Counterargument: explain how the opposition is limited or flawed.

Explain the value of your position.

- Explain how your position matters to others.
- Explain how your position best addresses the situation.

Argumentative assignments may ask writers to question a problematic term or phrase. For these arguments, writers start by defining the term or phrase as it is commonly used. They may ask how it shows up in writing and speaking. They may draw from a source or two to show specific usage. They might also explain its origin and how its use has changed over time. Then, they evaluate the term or phrase, asking what it gets wrong, how the term or phrase distorts or overly simplifies something. Finally, they explain the need for a new term or phrase, and what it might mean for thinkers and writers:

Examine a key term or phrase.

- Define the term or phrase.
- Explain how the term or phrase gets used.
- Refer to a source that uses the term or phrase.

Describe the inaccuracy of the term or phrase.

- Explain how the above definition is misleading.
- Explain how the above definition is incomplete.

Describe what the term or phrase conceals.

- Describe qualities that might be taken for granted.
- Describe effects that aren't immediately apparent.

Explain the need for a new term or phrase.

- Explain what function the new term or phrase would serve.
- Describe whom the new term or phrase would benefit.

Or writers can propose an actual change in terms. They begin by examining the original term or phrase, explaining what it gets wrong, how or why it's inaccurate. Then, they go a step further and describe the quiet associations that come along with the term or phrase. They explain how these associations misdirect people's thinking. Finally, they offer a new term or phrase, explaining how it prompts richer, more accurate, and more sophisticated thinking:

Examine a key term or phrase.

- Define the term or phrase.
- Explain how the term or phrase gets used.
- Refer to a source that uses the term or phrase.

Describe the inaccuracy of the term or phrase.

- Explain how the above definition is misleading.
- Explain how the above definition is incomplete.

Describe the associations of the term or phrase.

- Explain how the term or phrase reinforces a bias or prejudice.
- Explain how the term or phrase limits thinking.

Propose a new term or phrase.

- Define the new term or phrase.
- Explain how the new term or phrase is more accurate than the original.
- Describe the positive associations of the new term or phrase.
- Acknowledge any limitations of the new term or phrase.

Argumentative projects may ask writers to challenge the status quo or usual practices. Such projects can start by describing a real event or situation. Introductions give readers enough information to understand what has happened. Then, writers seek tension in the situation or event. They might ask what friction the situation or event calls to the surface. For this step, they may integrate a supportive source that characterizes the tension. They return to the original situation or event and explain how these quiet assumptions reinforce the status quo. Finally, they explain how this process has shown something interesting or new about the subject:

Describe a real situation or event related to the subject.
- Give details about the situation or event.
- Explain a subtle tension at play.

Describe a broad tension related to the subject.
- Use specific language to describe the tension.
- Integrate a source that describes the tension.

Describe quiet assumptions related to the subject.
- Explain how the quiet assumptions reinforce a bias.
- Explain how the quiet assumptions limit thinking.

Explain the value of your position.
- Explain how your position matters to others.
- Explain how your position best challenges or abandons the status quo.

Such an argument can also begin by questioning a maxim related to the topic. In this case, the writer begins by drawing attention to the reasoning behind the maxim, then explaining what it misses or gets wrong. A vital source may help to explain the problem with the maxim. Then, the writer may call out quiet assumptions that get reinforced by the maxim, explaining how those assumptions misdirect thinking. Finally, they explain why their position on the subject matters:

Question a maxim related to the subject.
- Explain how the maxim is inaccurate.
- Explain how the maxim is misleading or limited.

Draw from a vital source.
- Describe how the source relates to the maxim.
- Describe how it helps to show some logical flaw or shortcoming in the maxim.

Describe quiet assumptions related to the subject.

- Explain how the quiet assumptions reinforce a bias.
- Explain how the quiet assumptions limit thinking.

Explain the value of your position.

- Explain how your position matters to others.
- Explain how your position best challenges or abandons the logic of the maxim.

Reflective Projects

These projects get writers inside their own thinking. The goal is for writers to focus on their own progress, their struggles, and breakthroughs as they relate to particular writing assignments. Reflective projects include reflective memos and essays, literacy narratives, cultural identity projects, and critical memoirs. The following outlines illustrate common approaches. They rely on moves described in Chapter 1, "Seeking Complexity"; Chapter 3, "Analyzing Arguments"; Chapter 4, "Justifying a Position"; Chapter 6, "Seeking Tension"; Chapter 7, "Inspecting the Terms"; and Chapter 9, "Reflecting."

Reflection is often prompted by a real situation or event that gets writers focused on their own thinking. These projects start by describing the situation or event. Then, they seek tension in the situation or event. They may explain friction between what the writer expected and what the writer experienced. The writer may describe past assumptions about the subject and why they were limiting or flawed. This step might involve describing any dualities at work and how they hid interesting or valuable gray areas. Finally, a conclusion may return to the original situation or event and explain how the writer's thinking changed.

Describe a real situation or event related to the subject.

- Give details about the situation or event.
- Explain a subtle tension at play.

Examine past assumptions about the subject.

- Explain where the assumptions come from.
- Explain how the assumptions are flawed or biased.

Bust up a duality.

- Describe the duality: on the one side, there's _____, and on the other, there's _____.
- Explain how the duality is misleading or limited.
- Describe the gray area: between the two extremes, there's another possibility: _____.

Explain how you see the subject differently.

- Explain why it matters to those involved.
- Explain what new questions or problems emerge.

Reflective projects often reveal broad tensions that writers struggle with, often on a personal level. They may start by explaining the various layers of the tension—any historical, philosophical, or political friction at play. They may even integrate a supportive source that characterizes the tension. Then, the writers may examine past assumptions about the subject, considering how they've influenced thoughts or behavior. This can also involve seeking complexity in the subject and examining the quiet associations that were overlooked in the past. Finally, the conclusion explains how this reflection process has changed the writer's thinking:

Describe a broad tension related to the subject.

- Use specific language to describe the tension.
- Integrate a source that describes the tension.

Examine past assumptions about the subject.

- Explain where the assumptions come from.
- Explain how the assumptions are flawed or biased.

Describe the quiet associations of the subject.

- Describe qualities that might be taken for granted.
- Describe effects that aren't immediately apparent.

Explain how you see the subject differently.

- Explain why it matters to those involved.
- Explain what new questions or problems emerge.

11 Assessing the Moves

Countless studies and years of collective wisdom reinforce some basics about writing assessment. Despite different theoretical perspectives, grade level, and institution, teachers have come to agree on a few key elements: Assessment must be stitched into instruction. It should not be a separate language, one only teachers know and use. In other words, students should know the discourses of assessment—terms, phrases, and criteria that shape how writing gets evaluated. Students should, in fact, feel comfortable using assessment tools as they learn, practice, and revise their own writing. In practical terms, this means grading rubrics should include terms and phrases that show up on assignments and activity prompts. All those documents should align and cohere so students are not surprised when grading rubrics show up.

Cohering instruction and assessment is especially important when it comes to the intellectual or epistemic qualities of writing—those that are characterized as *richness, depth, sophistication, rigor,* and so on. As this book has argued, that dimension of writing is consistently the most valued (by teachers) and the most elusive (to students and teachers). The chapters, then, have proposed strategies for making student writing richer, deeper, and more sophisticated. For sound assessment practices, those strategies and associated terms should then show up in rubrics. The following sample rubrics offer ways to evaluate assignments while integrating terms from the earlier chapters.

Of course, the rubrics are broad enough to address assignment types. They do not include specific topics. They could, however, be amended according to classroom particulars. They all begin with assignment elements and then move on to other qualities. In each case, the first two sections rely on terms from Chapters 1–9. Categories are not weighted. In other words, this section does not offer strategies for enumerating each criterion. Such values would likely come from department or institution learning outcomes. However, it's worth noting that such rubrics are often weighted in favor of the initial two categories. For instance, teachers consistently put more value on Argument and Sophistication (see below) than Arrangement and Grammar.

I. Argumentative Writing

Argumentative assignments vary widely. The first category in each case rubric below identifies the assignment elements, the basic ingredients of the project. Essentially, the first category measures the appropriateness of the task: did the student understand and engage with the assignment? The second category gets to the qualities discussed throughout this book.

Assignment Type: Arguing a Public Issue

Argument

- The position is justified with sound reasons.
- Reasons are supported with sufficient evidence and/or outside sources.

- The writer engages opposing positions in counterarguments.
- The writer includes concessions and qualifiers when appropriate.

Sophistication
- The writer seeks complexity by unpacking terms, making comparisons, asking focused questions, creating context, and/or denying usual associations.
- The writer describes subtle tension between or within positions
- The writer draws from vital sources for crucial points.
- Where appropriate, the writer goes further by calling out quiet assumptions, questioning maxims, questioning logic, or busting up dualities.

Arrangement
- Paragraphs focus on individual reasons or forms of evidence.
- Opposition is managed in turnabout paragraphs.
- Transitions are provided where appropriate.

Grammar/Mechanics
- The writing follows grammatical conventions.
- Sentences are edited for clarity and coherence.
- The writing follows guidelines for usage and punctuation.
- The project is formatted according to assignment guidelines.

Assignment Type: Problem Solving Argument
Argument
- The problem is sufficiently described.
- The writer's solution is justified with sound reasons.
- Reasons are supported with sufficient evidence and/or outside sources.
- The writer engages opposing solutions in counterarguments.
- The writer includes concessions and qualifiers when appropriate.

Sophistication

- The writer seeks complexity by unpacking terms, making comparisons, asking focused questions, creating context, and/or denying usual associations.
- The writer describes subtle tension between or within positions.
- The writer draws from vital sources for crucial points.
- Where appropriate, the writer goes further by calling out quiet assumptions, questioning maxims, questioning logic, or busting up dualities.

Arrangement

- Paragraphs focus on individual reasons or forms of evidence.
- Opposition is managed in turnabout paragraphs.
- Transitions are provided where appropriate.

Grammar/Mechanics

- The writing follows grammatical conventions.
- Sentences are edited for clarity and coherence.
- The writing follows guidelines for usage and punctuation.
- The project is formatted according to assignment guidelines.

II. Analytical Writing

Analysis assignments tend to fall into two major categories: argument analysis and literary analysis. Teachers often ask students to inspect either a written argument (an article, essay, blog post, op-ed, etc.) or a literary work (novel, story, poem, etc.).

Assignment Type: Argument Analysis

Analysis

- The writer accurately summarizes the target argument, describing its main claim, reasoning, and evidence.
- The writer explains the role of the writer/speaker and their purpose.

- The writer explains the role of context, publication, and audience if appropriate.
- The writer explains counterarguments, concessions, and qualifiers within the argument.

Sophistication
- The writer seeks complexity by unpacking terms, making comparisons, asking focused questions, creating context, and/or seeking out unstated reasons.
- The writer describes subtle tension between or within positions
- The writer draws from vital sources for crucial points.
- Where appropriate, the writer goes further by calling out quiet assumptions, detecting subtle tension, and so on.

Arrangement
- Paragraphs focus on individual rhetorical elements or specific passages.
- The introduction characterizes the argument and summarizes it succinctly.
- The conclusion reinforces a key insight developed through close inspection of the argument.
- Transitions are provided where appropriate.

Grammar/Mechanics
- The writing follows grammatical conventions.
- Sentences are edited for clarity and coherence.
- The writing follows guidelines for usage and punctuation.
- The project is formatted according to assignment guidelines.

Assignment Type: Literary Analysis
Literary Elements
- The writer applies concepts (protagonist, plot, setting, etc.) related to the literary work.

- The writer goes beyond identifying elements to explain how they function in the work.
- The writer makes a distinct claim about a specific element of the literary work.

Sophistication

- The writer seeks complexity by unpacking terms, making comparisons, asking focused questions, and/or creating context for the literary work.
- The writer describes subtle tension between or among literary elements
- The writer draws from vital sources for crucial points.
- Where appropriate, the writer goes further by calling out quiet assumptions, transporting concepts, and so on.

Arrangement

- Paragraphs focus on individual literary elements or passages.
- The introduction characterizes the literary work and summarizes it succinctly.
- The conclusion reinforces a key insight developed through close inspection of the work.
- Transitions are provided where appropriate.

Grammar/Mechanics

- The writing follows grammatical conventions.
- Sentences are edited for clarity and coherence.
- The writing follows guidelines for usage and punctuation.
- The project is formatted according to assignment guidelines.

III. Personal/Reflective Writing

Personal writing is often narrative in nature. Students are prompted to tell personal stories and reflect on meaning or significance. Another important personal assignment is the writer's reflection, which often accompanies final projects or end-of-term portfolios.

Assignment Type: Personal Narrative

Narrative
- The narrative focuses on a key event or issue in the writer's life.
- The narrative is paced to maximize focus on that key event or issue.
- The writer discovers meaning or significance in that event or key issue.

Sophistication
- The writer seeks complexity by unpacking terms, making comparisons, asking focused questions, creating context, denying usual associations, questioning common reasons, and so on.
- The writer describes subtle tension when possible.
- When appropriate, the writer goes further by calling out quiet assumptions, questioning maxims, questioning logic, or busting up dualities.

Arrangement
- Paragraphs focus on individual moments or key scenes.
- The introduction brings the reader into a key moment of the story.
- The conclusion reinforces the meaning or significance of the key event or issue.
- Transitions are provided where appropriate.

Grammar/Mechanics
- The writing follows grammatical conventions.
- Sentences are edited for clarity and coherence.
- The writing follows guidelines for usage and punctuation.
- The project is formatted according to assignment guidelines.

Assignment Type: Writer's Reflection

Reflection

- The reflection focuses on specific assignments and/or passages.
- The reflection explains how specific assignments and/or passages operated within the whole (the term, the project, the writer's own development).
- The writer examines past assumptions—or those operating throughout the projects.
- The writer describes new thinking that emerged from the reflection.

Sophistication

- The writer seeks complexity by unpacking terms, making comparisons, asking focused questions, creating context, denying usual associations, questioning common reasons, inspecting terms, and so on.
- The writer describes subtle tension when possible.
- Where appropriate, the writer goes further by calling out quiet assumptions, questioning maxims, questioning logic, or busting up dualities.

Arrangement

- Paragraphs focus on passages, assignments, or moments throughout the process.
- The introduction explains the scope of the reflection.
- The conclusion reinforces new thinking that emerged from the process.
- Transitions are provided where appropriate.

Grammar/Mechanics

- The writing follows grammatical conventions.
- Sentences are edited for clarity and coherence.
- The writing follows guidelines for usage and punctuation.
- The project is formatted according to assignment guidelines.

Glossary of Moves

Adopting a Position and Purpose: Clarifying a specific point and intention for a written argument. The writer narrows down the particular assertion and goal of the argument. (See Chapter 4, "Justifying a Position.")

Adopting Specific Language: Borrowing words and phrases from a formal definition and using them in a specific application. The writer uses the formal definition of a concept to make sense of a specific topic, event, or text. (See Chapter 2, "Applying a Concept.")

Analyzing the Audience: Detecting and explaining the intended readership of a given argument. When analyzing an argument, the writer describes the values, beliefs, and/or interests of the intended audience. This description may include the publication or publication type. (See Chapter 3, "Analyzing Argument.")

Analyzing the Reasoning: Explaining the specific logical steps that lead to an argumentative claim (or thesis). When analyzing an argument, the writer describes each idea—each fact or belief—that must be accepted along the path to a final claim. (See Chapter 3, "Analyzing Argument.")

Analyzing the Writer/Speaker: Detecting and explaining a writer or speaker's purpose. When analyzing an argument, the writer describes the specific purpose of the author. (See Chapter 3, "Analyzing Argument.")

Applying a Supportive Source: Integrating an outside published source into an argumentative or informative project. When working with sources, writers stitch in others' language to reinforce their own claims and connect those claims to a wider world of thinkers and researchers. (See Chapter 5, "Applying Sources.")

Breaking Down Reasons: Articulating all the reasons for an argumentative claim (thesis). When making an argument, the writer spells out each belief that leads to a main claim. When linked together, these beliefs provide the justification for the argument. (Chapter 4, "Justifying a Position.")

Breaking Up Common Comparisons: Explaining the flaw in a widely used comparison. Writers can show the problems with an analogy, simile, or metaphor that has become normal and widely accepted. (See Chapter 8, "Escaping the Status Quo," Advanced Move.)

Breaking Up Dualities: Discovering a third option or category when only two opposites seem available. Writers can seek and describe alternatives beyond usual contrasting pairs. They can show the gray area between black and white. (See Chapter 6, "Seeking Tension," Advanced Move.)

Calling Out the Quiet Argument: Explaining what a nonverbal thing argues. The writer considers an object, event, photograph, work of art, or situation and explains how the specific elements add up to an argumentative claim. (See Chapter 3, "Analyzing Argument," Advanced Move.)

Calling Out Unstated Reasons: Explaining the unstated logical steps that lead to an argumentative claim (or thesis). When analyzing an argument, the writer describes each idea—each fact or belief—that must be accepted along the path to a final claim. Part of that process may involve describing facts or beliefs that are assumed but not directly worded in the argument. (See Chapter 3, "Analyzing Argument," Advanced Move.)

Challenging Quiet Assumptions: Questioning or arguing against an unstated belief. Writers can challenge widely accepted beliefs, even when those beliefs are considered normal or common sense. (See Chapter 8, "Escaping the Status Quo.")

Changing the Lens: Re-seeing a topic from a different perspective. Writers frame a topic so it is understood differently. They bring a new dimension to light or show an alternative side of the topic. (See Chapter 7, "Inspecting the Terms.")

Citing Sources: Attributing information or language to a particular source. When working with outside sources, writers must connect specific information (facts, statistics, testimony, theories, history, and so on) to the specific source that brought it forward. (See Chapter 5, "Applying Sources.")

Connecting to a Broader Tension: Linking a specific form of tension or intellectual conflict with a more general tension. Once writers sense something is out of sync, they can connect the particular with something widely established or widely understood form of conflict. (See Chapter 6, "Seeking Tension.")

Considering the Context: Acknowledging the impact of surrounding factors on a given argument. When analyzing an argument, the writer explains how social, political, or environmental trends may have shaped the nature of the claims. (See Chapter 3, "Analyzing Argument.")

Creating Context: Explaining the most important factors surrounding an issue. The writer selects relevant social, political, or environmental trends and explains how they have shaped the topic under consideration. (See Chapter 1, "Seeking Complexity.")

Denying the Usual Associations: Separating two ideas that are typically paired. The writer removes a term that usually gets associated with another and thereby reveals something distinct or surprising about the remaining term. (See Chapter 1, "Seeking Complexity," Advanced Move).

Detecting Inaccuracy: Explaining how a term or phrase gets misused or misapplied. Writers can argue about the accuracy or proper use of a term or phrase. The argument can explain what the term or phrase gets wrong, what it distorts or misses. (See Chapter 7, "Inspecting the Terms.")

Detecting Quiet Associations: Describing the unstated ideas that accompany specific terms. Writers can detail any/all ideas that come along with common words or phrases. The process might uncover some ideas that should be questioned. (See Chapter 7, "Inspecting the Terms.")

Detecting Subtle Tension: Explaining the difference between expectations and observations. Writers can describe the gap between what they expected and what they have actually witnessed. The gap may raise interesting questions about flawed expectations or the complexities of real events. (See Chapter 6, "Seeking Tension.")

Drawing from the Past: Referencing a source or author from a bygone era. Writers can borrow insights from historical sources, authors from past decades or centuries who make timeliness claims that still underscore important and relevant insights. (See Chapter 5, "Applying Sources.")

Drawing from a Vital Source: Borrowing key insights from a highly relevant and thorough source. When working with sources, writers often rely on an especially powerful source by circling back to key ideas/language. The vital source's language, always quoted and attributed, becomes a driving element. (See Chapter 5, "Applying Sources.")

Describing New Thinking: Expressing a better, newer, aspect of one's own beliefs. In a self-reflective passage, writers can describe how they have revised their own thinking. (Chapter 9, "Reflecting.")

Examining Past Assumptions: Explaining the flaw or shortcoming in a personal belief. Writers can admit their own intellectual development and describe how they discarded some previous way of thinking. (Chapter 9, Reflecting.)

Flipping the Terms: Suggesting the opposite of a widely used term or phrase. Writers can propose that the contrary idea might be more accurate, more helpful, more interesting. (See Chapter 7, "Inspecting the Terms," Advanced Move.)

Focusing the Questions: Asking the most narrow and specific questions possible. As an invention (prewriting) technique or as part of a formal essay, the writer asks probing questions about specific events, people, or phenomena. (See Chapter 1, "Seeking Complexity.")

Identifying Counters, Concessions, Qualifiers: Explaining how an argument deals with opposing positions or claims. When analyzing an argument, the writer identifies passages that refute opposing positions (counterargument), grants value to opposing positions (concession), and admits limits to claims (qualifiers). (See Chapter 3, "Analyzing Argument.")

Making New Comparisons: Linking two topics that are not typically linked. The writer finds some connection between two events, groups, objects, or places and describes what that connection suggests. (See Chapter 1, "Seeking Complexity.")

Managing Opposition: Acknowledging and engaging the complexities of opposing claims while maintaining one's own argumentative position. When making an argument, writers can refute opposition (in counterargument), grant value to some opposition (in concession), and admit the limits to their own claims (in qualifiers). (See Chapter 4, "Justifying a Position.")

Proposing a Different Term: Offering a new term or phrase to replace another. After pointing out the problem or inaccuracy of a widely used term, writers can suggest something more accurate. (See Chapter 7, "Inspecting the Terms.")

Providing Evidence: Integrating facts, statistics, and/or testimony for a given claim. When making an argument, the writer includes forms of evidence not only for the argument's main claim (thesis) but also for relevant reasons. (See Chapter 4, "Justifying a Position.")

Questioning Common Reasons: Challenging widely accepted reasons or the normal way of doing things. Writers can analyze and discover flaws in common sense—and in the ways common sense gets defended. (Chapter 8, "Escaping the Status Quo.")

Questioning Maxims: Challenging a widely used and familiar statement. Writers need not accept the standard wisdom that comes on old statements or proverbs. They can argue that some forms of wisdom should be questioned. (See Chapter 8, "Escaping the Status Quo.")

Seeking Reasons for Reasons: Detecting and explaining the justification for stated reasons in an argument. When making an argument, writers can dig further into their own reasoning and characterize any rationale for their reasoning. (See Chapter 4, "Justifying a Position," Advanced Move.)

Synthesizing Sources: Integrating two or more sources into a single written project. Writers bring various sources into the same project and orchestrate the different voices. (See Chapter 5, "Applying Sources.")

Taking on the Big Concepts: Applying a complex concept to specific topic, event, or text. The writer devotes a full paragraph, or more, to describing the concept under consideration. Part of that description makes a distinct comparison, which personalizes the writer's take on the concept. (See Chapter 2, "Applying a Concept.")

Transporting a Concept: Borrowing a concept from a different field of study and applying it to a specific situation, event, or text. The writer uses a concept from another discipline (e.g., mathematics, biology, religion, business, literary arts) and explains what interesting dimension that concept helps to show. (See Chapter 2, "Applying a Concept," Advanced Move.)

Trusting But Verifying: Determining the reliability of information in sources. Writers must decide on the soundness of information or claims within outside sources. They can make determinations by tracking the presentation of information. (See Chapter 5, "Applying Sources.")

Unpacking Broad Terms: Explaining many smaller aspects or ingredients of a broader term. The writer can use this move to avoid the reliance on vague words and phrases. Or the writer can list the smaller ingredients of a broad term directly in a formal passage. (See Chapter 1, "Seeking Complexity.")